Own YOUR Dreams

HOW TO TAKE POSSESSION OF THE LIFE YOU DESERVE

DR. ONA BROWN

CO-AUTHORED BY KAREN ANDRE JD • PAMELA KAWADA JD, ESQ
KARIM ELLIS • PATRICK TYRANCE, JR. MD

DANIELLE ROCCO • JEROME MALDONADO • MARK ANTHONY KING • DARWIN LIU
CAROL FEELEY ALINA UGAS • LUIS BOLINAO • STACEY RANDOLPH • PAUL WHITE
HILLARY FOSTER • DR. CHERYL D. GEORGE • CYNTHIA DALES • HAZIQ ALI
CHARLES TCHORERET • JENNIFER EVANS • PATRICK BROWN

Brown Family
PUBLISHING

OWN YOUR DREAMS: HOW TO TAKE POSSESSION OF THE LIFE YOU DESERVE

For permissions contact: info@brownfamilypublishing.com and www.ownyourdreamsnow.com

Published by Brown Family Publishing

ISBN: 978-1-7327450-1-8

Second Edition: June 2020

To my baby brother, Chad Marcus Williams, who earned his wings and left this life at the age of 16 years young. You will live on in my heart... I love and miss you dearly!

To the Dream Owners of the world who have the heart & boldness of a warrior and are pushing forward towards the full manifestation of their dream reality! We honor you and we salute you! Thank you for being who you are!

Finally, to those that are still working hard to bring out their voice... to discover their purpose and to keep their head up. You may have taken some tough hits in life... but you are still here for a reason. Don't you dare give up... lock arms with somebody... and hold on... until you find your way... you've got this...

YOU HAVE GREATNESS WITHIN YOU!!!

OWN YOUR DREAMS!!!

Table of Contents

FOREWORD

*A*s a little boy, I can clearly remember wondering what it would be like to experience a life of freedom. To live like the lucky people who had big homes, fancy cars and traveled in planes with lots of money to spare. My mama, Ms. Mamie Brown, taught me the power of a dream. She believed in OWNING dreams and taking action steps to make them become a reality. In spite of being a young, single woman of color, she dreamt of one day having children of her own, even though according to society she did not meet the required qualifications in order to adopt children.

However, she didn't allow someone else's opinion to block her progression. She believed with all of her heart that it was possible and that a way to make it happen would be revealed. Ultimately, she attracted the desires of her heart; my twin brother Wesley, my other adopted siblings and I are the results of hard work and answered prayers.

My mother's determination taught me to imagine what life would be like as a high achiever with success on my side. In my mind, rich people were worry free, stress free and drama free, which is what I wanted for myself and my family... an easy life... much like the soul soothing song "Easy Like Sunday Morning" that the great Lionel Richie so gracefully sang!

I was truly HUNGRY to live the life of my dreams, which is why I invested so much of my time living boldly and working tirelessly to experience the success that I wanted and yearned for on a daily basis.

In many ways, I attained the impossible and helped millions of others to do the same. BUT...

It didn't happen the way I thought it would. Life is never without problems, obstacles, and occasional setbacks that come out of nowhere.

Even when you are committed to living a life of greatness... it does not make you exempt from the misfortunes of life. Hard times, difficult people, and unexpected circumstances will find a way to visit you or someone you love.

Because life is filled with tests and twists that we must grow through to make our dreams become a reality. Who you are in the midst of a storm, determines what type of life you will be able to design for yourself. That is why giving up is not an option for success.

The great Reverend Dr. Johnnie Colemon, a powerful spiritual leader from the southside of Chicago, was well known for a very profound and thought-provoking quote, "It works, if YOU WORK IT!"

This collaborative self-development tool it just that... shared insights and wisdom that can help you to make your life, family and vision work. It is power-packed with soul-stirring stories and heart-warming heroism.

You will gain example after example of what dream ownership looks like, in a very up-close and personal way. May this work inspire, ignite, and recharge a burning desire within you and help you to remove all of the limiting beliefs that may be holding you and your dream hostage.

I am truly proud of my lovely daughter, Dr. Ona Brown, aka 'The Message Midwife' for creating this mind-expanding group of lights who spread vision, hope, power, and greatness by the telling of their stories.

I am also honored to be her father and the one she chose to write the foreword for this book. My children and grandchildren are the greatest blessings in my life, and they continually stretch me to keep dreaming new dreams and then to go after those dreams with a sense of urgency.

You were designed to be a Dream Owner. All you have to do is open your mind to the belief that it is possible for you. Once you learn how to breathe life into a vision in order to fully manifest and OWN your own dreams, you will NEVER be the same again. You were created to create something great in this life, and the world is waiting on it. You are indeed a masterpiece because you are piece of the master.

Keep this body of work close to you, reread/revisit it often, and share it with as many people as possible. This world will be an amazingly better place once we awaken the greatness within all of humanity. Keep love in your heart, and always remember to...
OWN Your Dreams.

Mr. Les Brown
Ms. Mamie Brown's Baby Boy
Global Speaker, Fortune 100 Trainer & Speaker Coach
www.iamhungrylesbrown.com

CHAPTER 1

Rise to the Occasion
by Dr. Ona Brown

*M*y Dad, Mr. Les Brown, taught me to dream big and then to press toward that dream with every fiber of my being until it becomes true. My life has been filled with amazing experiences because of the divine wisdom that both my Dad and Mom taught me. Because of who they chose to be... I am granted permission to be who I am!

Have you ever heard about an opportunity and you were so filled with such excitement that your entire spirit leaped? When something is in total alignment with your heart's desire and you just know that you have to do it. Well, that unexpectedly happened to me one day.

I was spending some time with a dear friend of mine, Reverend Kevin Ross, who told me about a trip he was going to take with a delegation of ministers from Chicago to Cape Town, South Africa. He was incredibly excited and the more he spoke about it, the more I realized this was a trip for me as well! When I told him I wanted to go, he said "Really?" and I said, "Yes, I definitely want to go." He thought that was a cool idea and told me he would make the request known with the president of the delegation and see if it was possible for me to go and get back to me with the outcome as soon as possible.

A couple of days later, he came back with the good news that the president was happy to have me come along, and all I had to do was cover my own expenses. I was so excited until he began to list out the expenses: round-trip flight from Chicago to Cape Town, five-star hotel for two weeks, food, and incidentals. Expenses started adding up fast. The number kept going up and up, and I thought, "Oh my goodness, how am I going to do this?"

Then I remembered what The Great Les Brown says,

*"Always remember that how is none of your
business. Just set the intention."*

Based upon that wisdom, I started doing what I knew how to do as an entrepreneur. At that time, I had a book of affirmations called *Affirmacise: 101 Affirmations for Daily Living* that shows people how to step into the gymnasium of their mind to affirm true power, love, peace, joy, and prosperity. I was selling the book, signing up coaching clients, consulting, conducting trainings and taking on speaking engagements at a breathless pace. Each time I made some money... I would get closer to my required goal. However, it seemed like with every progression, I would take three steps forward and then five steps back. Have you ever felt that way?

Every time I thought I was getting ahead, something else would happen that needed my attention, a crack in my car windshield, a flat tire or a broken furnace in the dead of winter. These various circumstances kept coming up and I began to feel defeated and doubtful.

Down to the Wire

I realized that I was getting down to the wire of when all of the required funds would be due and my hard-earned stashed amount wasn't even close to what it needed to be. So, I had to do the unthinkable. I had to make the most humbling call ever to my Pops and ask him for money.

All of my brothers and sisters will agree that asking our Dad for money is something that we try to avoid as much as possible. We don't want to have to do it because we already know what the lecture will consist of, "You have not tapped into your greatness, you are working with a poverty consciousness, and you are not fulfilling your true divine purpose because you are out of alignment with who you are designed to be and that's why you need to borrow money,"

As a result, that was a call that I did not want to make, but I felt like my back was up against the wall and time was ticking away along with this amazing opportunity. So, I took a deep breath and dialed his number and, initially, I only got his voicemail. I knew his number was a helpline for people from all over the world, and most of them called with a specific need, expectation, or request. It was not out of the ordinary for my Dad's voicemail to be full.

I thought to myself, "How am I going to get my request to the top? How am I going to stand out in this sea of people that have a need?" The solution was easy: I called back to back, to back, to back and filled up his voicemail with about twenty messages. He had no way to receive a message from anyone else because I filled it up with messages like, "Mr. Brown, this is your daughter. I need you to call me as soon as possible." "Hey Dad, call me, it's Ona." "Hey, how are you? I know I just left seven messages, but this is Ona. Please call me as soon as you get a chance."

After what seemed like an eternity, he finally called me and said, "Ona, what is going on? I can't get messages from anyone else except you. What could possibly be going on?"

I said, calmly, "That's a very good question. I'm so glad that you asked me that." (I knew that it had to be perfect, so I had practiced what I was going to say.) "Dad, I want to talk to you about an opportunity that we have to take advantage of. It's a beautiful experience that will not just impact my life and yours, but even the lives of those yet unborn."

"What are you talking about?" my father asked.

"There is a delegation of ministers going to Cape Town, South Africa, and I have been inspired to go with them. I know this is a part of my unfolding destiny. There is a huge gap between the amount of money that it takes to go on this trip and the amount of money that I currently have in my account. I want to talk to you, Mr. Brown, about how we can work together to close this big gap, and because of how I love you, I am willing to let you in on this huge opportunity."

"What are you saying?" he said.

"I don't have enough money to go to Cape Town, and I really need to go. Please, please, please, can you help me?"

His reply was simple, "Ona, I love you. I believe in you. I know you can make it happen." Click.

I wound up sitting there holding the phone and thinking to myself, "I know you did not just hang up on me. I know I'm not listening to the dial tone." But he was gone.

That's when the negative inner voice took over: "What made you think you could go? What made you think you were at a level to be able to do this? Obviously, you are not that successful. You're too big for your britches, and these are highly successful people that have thousands of dollars sitting around to do these types of things. What made you think you were worthy of this opportunity? You must be delusional; this makes absolutely no sense. Now you've embarrassed yourself. You've got to go back and tell the guy that you can't do it. Dad always said, 'How is none of your business,' but I guess it's your

4

business now because your dad just hung up on you." (frightened laughter)

How do you deal with that negative inner talk and conquer it, so it has no power over you? You say, "Thank you for sharing," and then don't allow it to take control of your mind. Keep pressing forward. Hold on to the vision of what you want.

For me to go on this trip, I realized I was going to have to implement everything I knew about self-development. It was time to raise the bar for myself, increase my daily internal work, and double my amount of affirmations, prayer, journaling, and visualization. It was time to exercise one of my favorite quotes:

> *"Feed your faith, and your fears will starve to death." – Unknown*

To do that, I needed to have a point of contact that would help me to know that it was already done. I decided to buy a globe so I could see and touch the point of Cape Town, South Africa, several times throughout the day. I also bought a dashiki shirt (which was a beautiful African garment made with vibrant colors) and wore it around the house as I was making coaching calls, seed calls, building my business, and reaching out for potential speaking engagements.

I did everything that I knew to do, and this helped to feed my faith and to raise my standards of expectation to know that it was possible, even though it seemed impossible – to see it in my minds eye as already done.

In the midst of me taking all of these powerful action steps, I got down to the final hour. During one of my meditations, it was revealed to me that I should make a gigantic move on behalf of my vision, something bold and courageous, and call my friend and ask him who the point of contact was for securing flights and hotel accommodations.

So I was obedient and called him, and he said, "Oh, that's a great question. There's a travel agent that we are all working with and she's handling the entire trip." I asked him for her contact information, and he gave it to me. I had no clue what I was doing, but I had to keep pressing forward. Sometimes when you're following your heart, you will feel a pull on your spirit; you may not know why you're doing it, but the key is to be obedient to your internal guide. I didn't know where this was going, but I called her and said, "How is everything coming along with the plans for the South African trip?"

She said, "It's going well. The delegation that you're supposed to be traveling with from Chicago are all on this particular plane, and it has only one seat left." I quickly proclaimed, "That seat is mine, please reserve it for me." I also instructed her to book me into the five-star hotel. "Now, Ms. Brown, will that be American Express, MasterCard, or Visa?"

"Oh. That's a great question. May I call you back with that information?" And she said, "Sure." Then I quickly got off the phone because I didn't know why she replied, "Sure." I'm thinking to myself, how is she going to hold the reservation without a credit card? That doesn't make any sense. I didn't have a card to give her at that moment, but this allowed me more time to make it happen.

So I kept doing what I knew how to do. I worked hard at securing new business to cover the cost. I kept building my faith with visualizations, meditating, praying, touching the globe, and wearing the dashiki, I also went and secured my passport as well. A couple of days later my friend, Rev. Kev, called and he asked me, "What type of God do you serve?"

I immediately responded, "I serve a great God. Why do you ask?"

He replied, "Well, I want to give you an update. The president of the delegation reached out to the travel agent to see where we were with completing the preparations for the South Africa trip. The travel agent told him (the president), 'We're doing pretty good. Everything is 99% complete, and all the T's are crossed except for one outstanding item. Ms. Brown doesn't have a card applied to her flight or hotel as of yet.' The president was fully aware of my fundraising efforts and then said, 'Since we are below budget for our portion of the trip, how about we just cover her in full.'"

I couldn't believe it. "Are you serious?"

"Yes, you are going to South Africa," he replied.

I jumped up and down, screamed and cried all at the same time. I was amazed and so happy and grateful. My heart was filled to the point of overflowing. We never know when or how the manifestation will happen. All of the preparation ahead of time fortified my faith and kept me moving forward. I set my intention, took massive action, and trusted that it would all work out.

A Trip That Turned into Something Incredible

When we landed in Cape Town, the experience was exquisite and surreal with the warm tropical heat and the peaceful presence that I felt upon arrival. I was glowing with joy and strutting with my head held high. I was the only female and non-minister on the trip, and all the men became big brothers, uncles, and grandfathers to me. They guided me and provided cover and protection. I was the baby sister who had been magically added to the trip, and nothing was going to happen to me.

We arrived at the five-star hotel, and the van door was pulled back by this gentleman who had gorgeous, rich, dark skin, and this amazing, wide smile with ivory white teeth, and he said to us, "Welcome home, my brothers and sisters, welcome home."

I thought to myself, "Oh, he must think we're from here. Why is he saying welcome home?" Then I had this revelation that we are the descendants of the ones that were taken away from here, so this is coming home for us. I was so overwhelmed with emotion that I burst into tears, and the ministers had to help to carry me into the hotel lobby. It was an unforgettable experience and I kept pinching myself to make sure that I wasn't dreaming.

While I was freshening up and getting ready for dinner, I realized I was in the middle of an experience that I had focused on creating for weeks. Then, a question came to my mind, "If I could do this, then anything is possible. What else would be amazing for me to accomplish while I am in this zone of manifestation?"

I had been around famous people for most of my life, but one person I always wanted to meet was the Honorable Nelson Mandela, and here I was in South Africa. Why don't I raise the bar even further and set a new intention to actually meet him before I leave South African soil?

I set my heart and intention on it. Then I started imagining it, writing it, and declaring it with my mouth because, like the Bible says, "Death and life are in the power of the tongue," and "You will also declare a thing, and it will be established for you; so light will shine on your ways." I told my friend that we're going to meet the Honorable Nelson Mandela, and he said, "How?" I answered, "How is none of our business."

We started asking everyone around if they happened to know where the Honorable Nelson Mandela hangs out, eats, and where he lives. Everyone told us that we couldn't meet him; that's impossible. My reply was, "You don't know how I got here because I already manifested one miracle, and so a second one is definitely possible. Your thinking is too limited for what I am working to accomplish, so you're not the person that I should be talking with."

Don't share your vision with everyone because there are people who are naysayers and naturally negative. They will bring their limited thinking to your vision and tell you why it can't happen.

By asking several people, we found out that Nelson Mandela would be speaking at a conference called, "The Parliament of the World's Religions" that I was also going to be attending. It was designed to bring down the walls that separate us and focus on how to end global poverty, disease, and war. Their goal was to make the world a better place by good people uniting and joining forces.

I was so excited, and one step closer to meeting Mr. Mandela. My friend wasn't as enthusiastic and said, "We don't even have the upgraded ticket to see him, and they are saying that it is completely sold out. How are we going to get in?"

"I don't know, but we will get in the building.'" I replied with confidence.

We went to the venue where he was speaking and stood in the crowd. I knew a miracle could happen, and I was waiting for it to be revealed. I didn't know when it was going to happen, but my faith was strong. I kept praying, "Let me be aware of what is going on, let me be in the present moment, let me be in tune with how this is going to unfold.

We started greeting people, and I heard someone say, "Ona?" I turned around; it was a minister that I knew from California, and I said, "Hi, how are you?"

"I am so out of it; and we are dealing with serious jetlag. My wife and I just arrived here from Brazil after days of travel. We're supposed to be a part of a group of people that presents an award to Nelson

Mandela, but we are exhausted. Could you help us get through the crowd, into the building and down to the front of the stage, please?"

"Of course, I can." My friend and I took their bags, and we became their instant armour-bearers, moving people out of the way, going, "Excuse me, excuse me, watch out, coming through. They're part of the group presenting the award to Nelson Mandela, and they have to get through to the front please."

I can't believe I made it inside and then all the way to the front row. They seated me next to his wife, and my friend went backstage to help him. The anticipation was rising to hear Nelson Mandela; you could feel it. Just as he was ready to be introduced, a woman walked up to me and said, "Are you Ona?" I said, "Yes," and she replied, "The minister asked that you and his wife come backstage and would like for you to be one of the twelve people who get to meet Mr. Mandela after he speaks and before they whisk him out of the building to his limo."

"Are you kidding me?"

"Nope, follow me."

I followed this woman dancing, singing, and crying all at the same time. We got backstage and went through security. I heard him addressing the audience and telling them about the power of peace and unity. The crowd was going wild. At the end, they gave him a standing ovation.

I was at the bottom of the steps he had to come down after leaving the stage. I opened my arms up as wide as I could, and I looked up at him and said, "NELSON, I LOVE YOU!" at the top of my lungs. And he hugged me with so much love and honor. It was one of the warmest hugs I have ever received. I was shaking and crying as we talked to each other eye to eye. He finished with, "Thank you. So nice to meet you."

When I share this story with my audiences, I tell them that it took everything I had at that moment not to propose, because any man that can go from prisoner to President – that's marriage material. I'm very proud of myself; I was decent, respectful, orderly, and did not propose to him. (blushing)

He spoke with the others backstage and we all prayed together. He then got into his limo and was gone. I was standing there with my mouth wide open, thinking to myself, "Did this just happen?" It felt like a dream. Now for the cherry on top. I went back to my hotel room, and I could not wait to call my Dad. He normally does not answer his phone, but my very nature demanded that he answer. He picked up the phone and said, "Ona, aren't you in South Africa?"

"Yes, I am here, but I wanted to let you know something. Not only did I manifest myself to Cape Town, I just met the Honorable Nelson Mandela."

"Are you serious? Did you say anything about me?"

"No, I did not. For some reason, you slipped my mind." When I tell audiences that, they burst into laughter.

I share this beautiful story with you not to impress you, but to impress upon you that there's so much more inside of you and it is up to you to rise above your self-imposed limitations. We often put ourselves in boxes of restriction and hold our visions, talents, gifts and dreams hostage. We have told ourselves what's possible and impossible, and the reality is that whatever your heart desires, whatever your dream might be, it *can* happen.

Decide what you really want. It may not be going to South Africa; it may be traveling the entire world and touching all seven continents, and maybe seeing the seven wonders of the world. Maybe you want to help young people and save them from dying at young ages because of gang violence, drugs or suicide. Maybe you desire to help people find their goals, find their dreams, and live out their passions. It might be that you want to become an amazing stay-at-home mom or CEO, or a top executive, or a best-selling author, a world-renowned singer, or a poet.

Whatever it is, you can own your dreams. Just remember these three things:

- The how is none of your business; just set the intention.
- Build your faith each day by visualizing, journaling, praying, declaring, and decreeing what you want to create with your life.
- Show your belief by taking action steps towards it, and don't let the words of others influence or discourage you.

When your dream has come true, don't forget the most important part to remember. Always remain grateful and make the commitment to teach someone else that is ready and willing to learn!

Growing in peace, love, power and gratitude,
Dr. Ona Love Brown,
'The Message Midwife'/ Coach/Brand Builder/ Visionary
Les Brown's Baby Girl

Dr. Ona Brown
aka The Message Midwife

Dr. Ona Brown is a leading international, personal and professional self-development expert who has been empowering people and organizations since 1995. She inspires and motivates audiences in hundreds of U.S. cities, as well as many locations abroad, including London, England; Sydney, Australia; Johannesburg & Cape Town, South Africa; Stockholm, Sweden; Singapore, Asia; Abu Dhabi, UAE and many more.

Through her consulting, coaching, and corporate training firm, World Impact Now (WIN), Dr. Ona helps people from all walks of life to break down their self-imposed, perceived barriers and tap into their own inner greatness. Also known as 'The Message Midwife' she helps individuals and groups to utilize the power of their voice and to give birth to their own unique message that is customized to share with the world.

Working with her father, Les Brown, a world-renowned motivational speaker, Dr. Ona was a secret ingredient behind the scenes of marketing, sales and business development for years. Finally, she rose to become the CEO of Les Brown Unlimited, which impacts millions of lives globally. Groomed for entrepreneurship and vision expansion, it was expected that Dr. Ona would eventually spread her wings to soar even higher, launching her own business, W.I.N., while still continuing to simultaneously consult for her father's business and share stages with Mr. Brown whenever their schedules permitted. She often states her intention and magnificent obsession as follows:

"I will somehow make the world better before taking my last breath!" – Dr. Ona Brown

"Life is filled with accelerated change, pressing challenges, and a boatload of choices. Now is the time to be authentic, be empowered, and reclaim your dream! Your dream ownership is authorized by YOU!"
– Dr. Ona Brown

Dr. Ona's wide array of content development includes numerous audio programs, courses and books, such as: How To Fall In Love With Your Life, Discovering the Greatest You, Maximize Your Talent & Multiply Your Money,

Own Your Dreams, Answer the Call, *and* When the Seasons Change. *Some of the highlights of Dr. Ona's achievements are being the proud recipient of an Honorary Ph.D. in Economic Development as well as the Presidential Award from the 2016 Obama Administration. She has been honored to be invited as the keynote speaker at Harvard University, Coca Cola, XEROX, United Way, American Airlines and at the Circle of Mothers, (a program supported by The Trayvon Martin Foundation.) Both, Buffalo, New York and New Orleans, Louisiana have dedicated an Ona Brown Day in their cities in appreciate for the great work that she has done and will continue to do.*

Dr. Ona Love Brown
'The Message Midwife'/Empowerment Coach/Brand Builder/Visionary
'Les Brown's Baby Girl'

Go to www.onabrown.com/book-ona/ to connect with Ona for your next event, conference, or training.

CHAPTER 2

Seize the Day
by Karen André, JD

*S*ome moments change your life forever. Carpe Diem, which is Latin for "seize the day," became my motto after a seminal event in New York City, Labor Day weekend, 2001. A family friend learned that I was in town and invited me to visit the world-famous Windows of the World restaurant at the World Trade Center. I had spent the day out and thanked him graciously and said, "Let's connect next time I am in the city."

Less than two weeks later, I watched with the world in horror as the Twin Towers collapsed. Thankfully, our family friend was not on-site that day, but that was my first reminder not to wait for "next time" or "someday."

Deciding early in life to live in high definition color and sound requires that I take action and some risks to engage in life fully, seize opportunities, and create memories. For me, life is not a hamster wheel; it is a magic carpet ride. The tapestry is woven from life's experiences. The brighter, bolder, and richer my life experiences are, the more vibrant the tapestry.

I wanted to look back over my life, dazzled by the rich array of experiences forming that tapestry of memories. I knew I would have to move and think differently and take risks to create the life of my dreams. That decision would set me on a path that would take me to the Obama White House.

I vividly recall the night that Barack Obama won the Iowa primary in 2008. I was on the phone with a fellow political junkie, pacing in my living room. I dared not dream of an outright victory but at least a solid and respectable showing. When he won, the political world was shaken. Not since Jesse Jackson had an African American presidential candidate reached a point of viability of that magnitude.

I became obsessed with his progress as the primaries heated up. Soon, I found myself volunteering and spending more time helping Barack Obama than tending to my fledgling law practice.

The year 2008 was a rough year for me as I struggled to keep a steady income flowing due to the stagnating economy. I had a mortgage, law school loans in the six figures, and was trying to manage a tumultuous relationship with my fiancé. The only thing that lit me up was tracking the progress of this impressive man, Barack Obama. It became my dream to serve in his historic campaign.

Without my knowledge, I was recommended for a campaign position by a Florida Obama campaign staffer, and a well-respected civic leader. They knew my reputation in the community and that I would put my heart and soul into the work.

In August, when I got "the call," the conversation was brief, *"Hello. I am the regional field director for the Obama campaign in Miami. Your name came to me from two highly respected sources and based on your resume, we know you are overqualified for this position. However, we desperately need someone with your talents, relationships, and Haitian Creole language skills to run our Little Haiti office. We do not mean to insult you; we are calling to offer you a job as a field organizer. If you want it, it's yours. However, there will be no days off until after the election on November 4th. We will work seven days a week, 12 to 16 hours per day. The pay is paltry, and we know that it can be a challenge. Please take a day or two to think about it, talk to your family, see if they can support you financially, and call me back to let me know your decision."*

The entry-level job was more a threat to my financial stability than a blow to my ego. Yet, I still found myself pondering the opportunity because I believed that Barack Obama had a strong chance of becoming the next President of the United States.

I knew his election would cause a seismic shift in American and global politics; I thought back to the civil rights era and its leaders who changed this nation. I pondered whether I would have taken up the banner for racial justice and equality if I had been alive then. The answer was a resounding, "Yes." I needed to get off the sidelines and take action.

Additionally, my first niece, Jada, was born in June of 2008. I wanted her and all children to grow up knowing that regardless of their beginnings, cultural background or gender, it is possible with hard work and dedication to make an immense political impact.

It is important to me that there can be no glass ceiling on what is possible; therefore, I decided I would do my part to shape history. I refused to look back in regret for failing to seize the day. I jumped in with both feet and never looked back. It was the best decision and the most nerve-racking, yet exhilarating experience of my life.

In August, I closed down my law office and went to work for Senator Obama's campaign in Little Haiti. By conventional standards, I was committing career suicide, but I had committed to living a life based on my values and the principle of seizing the day!

I was ready to shock the world by helping Barack Obama get elected president. History would not pass me by. I would have no regrets and leave it all on the field. I felt, "The fierce urgency of now," a Martin Luther King quote used by Senator Obama. No more someday. I was all in.

On my first day, I had to find a new office. The closest place I found to organize and work was in the back of a McDonald's. I would arrive early in the morning, set up my laptop, and meet with volunteers. There's a street adage that says, "Real recognizes real." Being unstoppable, resourceful, and determined showed the locals that the Obama staff was not afraid of hard work and would not be deterred from engaging with them in the heart of their community.

Before I knew it, in addition to Little Haiti, I was assigned to Liberty City. I never doubted I could do it, nor did it occur to me that I was getting paid one salary for two jobs. Other than the actual election results, the amazing friendships and relationships I made on the campaign trail were the best part of the entire experience. I met people from around the world of every color, language, and religion.

So many unconscious biases were dispelled on both sides as I connected heart-to-heart with people I might never have met otherwise. I made lifelong, real friendships with people of different races, ethnicities, viewpoints, and economic backgrounds. They have added immeasurable richness to the tapestry of my life.

Finally, our office opened. We got a celebrity surrogate, Dwyane Wade, the professional basketball player, to help! The neighborhood children were elated. The elders were pleased, and we kicked off the opening of the Liberty City office with a bang.

Simultaneously, a super volunteer named Ariel was running the Little Haiti office. Hers is one of the first cherished friendships born from this campaign that has lasted the decade since the election. In Liberty City, the late Daisy Black, mayor of a nearby town, helped every day as well. I could have never successfully managed two offices without these two women. The level of dedication shown by Ariel, Daisy, and countless other volunteers across the nation is what helped clinch the victory in 2008.

With both offices open, we began attracting volunteers in droves. Everyone in the community found a purpose, place, a home in the offices, and a greater mission. Everyone we met was feeling the electricity and generously giving of themselves to help seize the day! The magic created when people are inspired to say yes and risk disappointment for hope and change is indescribable.

We were building the community daily. Bobby, a proud community dad, brought local teenagers to earn community service hours even though they were too young to vote. Two local accountants, Vanessa and Robert, did daily data entry. The James', our newlyweds, were regulars and parents of our first Obama baby. Shana and Big Bert, proud Liberty City residents, were my eyes and ears in the community.

From the twelve Danish exchange students we dubbed "Danes for Change," to Francisco with the charming Italian accent – who rode his motorcycle from New York; to Spike Lee, who signed our office mural; to members of the British parliament who marveled at the electric atmosphere, our offices were a hit. A group of Delta Sigma Theta sorority sisters came from Alabama and enthusiastically convinced voters to stay in line by doing cheers and dance routines on hot, muggy days, and even when monsoon rains threatened voter turnout.

Driving past polling stations in the pouring rain, seeing lines out the door, around the corner, and down the street was a poignant moment. Voters waited patiently, covering themselves with umbrellas, and garbage bags – whatever it took.

Young black men whom society would see as hoodlums, protectively doted over seniors, providing chairs and water on sweltering hot days. Droves of young people joined the voter rolls to vote enthusiastically for the first time.

The night that Senator Obama accepted the Democratic nomination marked 45 years to the day that Martin Luther King delivered his famous speech at the March on Washington. The field staff was expected to organize a watch party in our campaign office. Instead, I got a company to erect a screen so that the community could watch it together in the local park. We seated the elders front and center to witness this historic moment. They all wept with joy. That night, the "never in my lifetime generation," could not believe their eyes.

There were even more tears on election night. Tears of disbelief, of joy, of sadness, remembering the painful past, tears for the ancestors that paved the way with their bodies so that we all could live and experience this moment. I shuttled between the two offices to celebrate with my volunteers and residents. Outside the Little Haiti office, a Haitian rara band was ready to lead the carnival procession down the streets in celebration.

The election was called long before I thought it would be. I stood there, blinking, trying to comprehend what I was hearing. When President Obama won easily, not only was the elation electric, but the relief coursing through my body was unforgettable. My risk had paid off! We had achieved the seemingly impossible. We made history!! It would take me some time to process the magnitude of that moment personally and societally.

When I returned to the Liberty City office, our six-foot Obama poster was floating down the street in some crazed celebrant's hands.

The neighborhood was rejoicing! I stood there beaming, watching the antics, and hugging my volunteers.

I looked over and saw two older gentlemen I knew and respected talking together. James was a political operative, and Mr. Pitts was a revered businessman and my office landlord. I can never reflect on that moment without shedding a tear. They stood, grasping shoulders, reminiscing about the days when they weren't allowed onto the public beaches in Miami. They recalled the days when they had to leave Miami Beach before sundown, enter buildings through the back door, and drink from "colored only" water fountains.

They wept loudly, releasing years of anguished pain, indignation, and hopelessness. An African descendant elected to be the President of the United States was something they never thought they would live to see. Their reaction mirrored that of a pensive, teary-eyed Jesse Jackson, watching President Obama's election night speech in Chicago's Grant Park.

The Cost Was Worth It

Suspending my law practice and life for the campaign resulted in an incredible, magical high but also brought unforeseen, incredible lows. My fragile relationship grew more strained during the all-consuming campaign, leading to an inevitable breakup shortly after the election.

Similarly, returning to my law practice in early 2009 was daunting as the nation was in the grips of a full-blown recession. I struggled to make ends meet, to keep my home during the mortgage crisis, and to heal from the breakup. It was a lonely and confusing time. Yet, I had no regrets.

I knew I was walking in my purpose. I was charting a new path for my life that required taking risks and walking by faith. I recognized that my challenges were merely growing pains that came with taking risks. When I grew anxious or discouraged, I reminded myself of what Henry Ford said, "Obstacles are those frightful things you see when you take your eyes off your goal." I had proudly tried my best to keep my eyes on the goal of living my core values and principles as I helped elect President Obama, despite the personal cost.

The New Call

That dedication was noted at the highest levels of the 2008 campaign. In the spring of 2011, I got "the call" again. My unwavering commitment to President Obama's politics was cited as a reason I was offered the role of Florida Deputy Political Director for President Obama's re-election. I had to pause and savor the full-circle moment. It affirmed all I knew to be true. When you show up to serve with an open mind and heart, people take notice.

Here is what I learned through this experience:

- Any dream involves risk, and you must be willing to move forward even when you're not sure of the result. Always be willing to take that next step.
- Commitment is the key to success. It will carry you past any obstacle you face.
- Do not determine your dream by the circumstances in front of you because they can easily change.
- Look for those who will help support you and make your dream come true.

I still marvel at the opportunities that opened for me on the campaign trail. The commitment to service and brave risk-taking carried me to Washington, D.C. in ways that still leave me speechless. I could never have scripted this journey, and I stand amazed at how one fateful decision to seize the day guided my life's trajectory, and I am so thankful!

Karen André, JD

Attorney Karen André, JD is the principal of The André Group and has dedicated her life to public service and advocacy. She recently served as Senior Advisor to Andrew Gillum in his primary win as Democratic nominee for governor of Florida in 2018. From 2014 to 2017, she served as a Presidential appointee in the Obama administration as the White House Liaison to the U.S. Department of Housing and Urban Development.

Ms. André has advocated for Haitian and African American communities on social justice issues including helping mobilize for the passage of the Haitian Refugee and Information Fairness Act (HRIFA).

As a testament to her service, Ms. André was named one of South Florida's 50 Most Powerful Black Professionals and one of 20 South Florida Freedom Sisters by the Ford Motor Company. Ms. Andre was also inducted into the Haitian Round Table's 1804 List of Haitian American Change-makers. In 2019, she was honored in the inaugural class of Next Generation Cultural Crusaders by the Ayiti Community Trust. Ms. André is a sought-after political strategist, professional speaker, and commentator. She holds a bachelor's degree in Psychology from Florida International University and a Juris Doctor from the University of Miami School of Law

CHAPTER 3

Design Your Destiny
by Pamela H. Kawada, JD Esq.

y grandmother had the most amazing, healing hands. Small
and freckled from the sun and age, her hands were soft and
warm, like a plush, stuffed teddy bear. Her gentle hands brushed my
long hair into a ponytail before I rushed off to play. Her strong hands
cooked many meals of bone marrow soup. The vegetables were
meticulously cut, and the soup was colorful, delicious, and filled with
love.

At the young age of twenty-five, my grandmother was living with
her husband in a traditional square Korean house. Her girls, ages two
and four, were playing near her when a frantic neighbor came to share
the awful news that my brave grandfather died in the war that had
enveloped Korea.

She was dazed and in shock. The stew on the wood stove came to
boil and overflowed, foreshadowing the emotions she would later feel.
The neighbor, with sympathetic tears rolling down her face, looked
into my grandmother's dazed eyes, then shook her gently back to
reality.

My grandmother then ran into the desolate rice fields, obliterated
by the war, looking for her husband and calling out his name. She

hoped that the news was not real and that he would respond and walk up to her still alive.

Soon, she saw his bloody hand, the same hand that once held hers. She would have recognized his hands anywhere. He was gone. She held her dead husband's body, cradling him like a baby. Immense tears ran down her face. Her body shook like the rumble of thunder as she simultaneously accepted and protested the tragedy of her life. She tried to scream at God, but her voice was empty, the pain so deep there was no sound.

Reality eventually hit, and she knew she had to say goodbye to the man she loved so deeply. The agony of letting go of their dreams was excruciating. She carefully laid his body back on the dirt. She looked up to the sky, and a ray of sunshine sprinkled warmth onto her numb face. It felt like a kiss from God. It was what she needed to keep living for her daughters. She saw her two daughters' sweet faces with their porcelain skin, rosy cheeks, and silky black hair smiling at her.

"I must make my daughters proud of me! I have to live! I MUST live!" she exclaimed as she pushed herself up. She stood tall as the wind blew her hair back. There was a fire inside my grandmother; a purpose, a yearning to live for her daughters. She knew that she would not only survive, but she would thrive!

A Spirit of Excellence

Rather than give up on life, my grandmother knew she had to support her daughters, and made the choice to move forward with her life. She thought about what her intrinsic talent was. As she looked down at her hands, she knew.

She started a business selling specialty blankets. Each one was uniquely and skillfully sewn for the customer with her gifted hands.

Each piece of fabric was imbued with good fortune and prosperity in a time that needed positivity.

She walked miles with her wares on top of her head, trying to sell the blankets door to door. As time went by, the blankets became popular amongst her village and neighboring towns. She became successful with her unique talents and charm. People gravitated towards the hope of a new life that the blankets brought and symbolized.

However, walking so much was taxing. She decided to have a store and house where customers could come to her. That made more sense. By designing and envisioning her goals and setting her intentions, she saved enough money and opened a store selling traditional Korean clothing called "hanbok," along with blankets of every variety. The store and home became a haven to raise her two children and eventually her grandchildren, including me!

My grandmother raised me from birth and after my mother passed. She raised me by herself to an even higher degree of excellence than she did her daughters.

For the eighty-six years my grandmother graced this earth, she molded me by her example of living a life of integrity. I learned that integrity is something no one can take away from you; it can't be bought or stolen because it is within you. Integrity guides you even when no one is watching.

She taught me that finding your purpose and moving toward your goals gives your life meaning, and that a deep and abiding faith carries you through whatever hardship and struggles you face. My grandmother always remained optimistic despite the many trials and tribulations she faced.

Living My Dreams

My grandmother's work ethic and beliefs led me to dream big. I knew that education would be integral to empowering myself and attaining my goal of becoming a lawyer.

It was hard at times, but I remembered how my grandmother would make a plan, keep focused on the goal, and work until it was done. This allowed me to graduate at the top of my class, Magna Cum Laude, Phi Betta Kappa with Honors from UCLA and immediately go to UCSF, Hastings College of the Law.

The competition was fierce, and I was faced with many challenges. I had to balance schoolwork and my family affairs. During law school, I was away from my grandmother, but had to balance time to see her and care for her as she was getting older and had medical issues. It was a lot of hard work and sacrificing of my personal time. Besides obligations to my family, I had to keep my attention on my academics. There wasn't time for much else. In the end, it was worth it as I made Hastings Law Review, the most competitive one there is.

While studying for the bar, I remembered my grandmother when it got difficult. I would think about how she managed to thrive under such difficult circumstances. If she could do it, then so could I, and I went back to my work.

When I was offered a corporate position at a prestigious international law firm in Los Angeles right after graduating, I knew it was worth it. I thought that one of my greatest challenges was behind me. Little did I know what was to come next.

Passing of the Torch

My grandmother became ill. It was so hard to see her deterioration start. Even though she was my grandmother, for me, she was more; she was my mother as well. When I looked at her, I didn't see an older woman. I saw the vibrant woman who had raised me with such strength and dedication. Now I was watching one of the people I loved most become weaker over time.

Even though the last years of her life were spent in and out of hospitals, she remained positive, always worrying about being a burden to others. She was always selfless, loving, and giving. It was hard to see the strongest force in my life becoming feeble.

A month before she passed, we were in the ICU at the hospital. I was pregnant at the time, and she was holding on to see her great-grandchild born.

Unfortunately, I had a miscarriage and was hoping she had forgotten I was pregnant. Her body may have been deteriorating, but her mind was still bright and sharp. Like a beautiful and fragrant rose, the petals were wilting, and I knew all of them would soon fall.

I sat by her bed with the illumination of the stark lights from all the hospital machines that kept her breathing. I looked at her with loving and adoring eyes and said, "Mama, I'm here!" as I held her baby-soft hands in mine.

She looked at me and squeezed my hand firmly. Then she asked where the sonogram of the baby was. I told her there was no picture, that I had lost the baby. She cried out to God, "Why did you take this baby away from my baby? Why, my dear Pamela?"

I laid my head on my grandmother's loving hands and said, "Mama, I'm okay. Please be okay, too. God has a plan, as you always tell me."

She placed her gentle hands on my face and said, "Yes, you are my child, faithful, loving, and strong!" That was the first and last time that I was the one giving her an example of the everlasting faith she had once taught me.

We embraced as she hummed a gospel song. Even though the room was sterile and as cold as a freezer box of ice, our hearts were warm; we were kindred spirits of life, of love, and loss.

A month later, my grandmother breathed her final breath. Now it was up to me to carry on her strength and legacy.

More Trials to Follow

I was able to get pregnant again after my grandmother died. It was bittersweet. I was keeping strong, but inside there was a deep hole in my heart. I longed to talk to her one more time, and I yearned to hold a baby I never would.

When I lost baby number two, it only deepened. For someone who had learned to take complete control of her life, these three losses shook me to the core. The only thing that got me through was remembering my grandmother. If she could let go after losing her husband in the war then I could heal from my loss.

It didn't happen all in one day, but I remember when I felt like I could see the light again. I had been torturing myself with the thoughts of how my babies died, and when I finally gave it over to God my body relaxed, and peace started to come in.

My next pregnancy was different. Miraculously, two years later, my son Sebastien was born the same day my grandmother passed away. He is a gift from God. I see my grandmother in my son's eyes. He has her optimism and an old soul, like hers. As my son lives and thrives, my grandmother lives through him.

When I hold my son's warm and sweet hands, I think of my grandmother's hands. The hands that cared for me so lovingly my entire life. The hands of wonder and grace. The hands of pure love and joy, whiter than a dove and sweeter than the purest lily of the valley; my grandmother's hands.

Now I get to pass down to my son and you the lessons I learned from her:

- Circumstances can never destroy you; they only make you stronger and better. You don't know what may be thrown your way, but the beauty comes from the journey and the life lessons learned.
- Be excellent in all you do. Diligence, perseverance, and optimism are the keys to making your dreams come true.
- God's love is all powerful, and if you let it in, it will heal and empower your heart.

The most valuable lesson I learned is that love conquers all. As you serve others, it comes back to you, and your dreams come true. When you get discouraged, remember my grandmother and Design Your Destiny!

Pamela H. Kawada, JD Esq.

Pamela H. Kawada, JD Esq.

Pamela H. Kawada, JD Esq. was born in Korea and immigrated to Los Angeles at four years old. The strong women in her life, her mother and her grandmother, taught her the importance of education, integrity, diligence, and faith. These lessons motivated her to graduate top in her class with Honors, magna cum laude, Phi Beta Kappa from UCLA.

After law school, Pamela worked as a corporate litigator at a prestigious international law firm in downtown Los Angeles. While there, she represented up to multi-billion-dollar companies in matters such as breach of contract, jurisdiction, and business strategy. An international traveler, she is passionate about lifestyle, fashion, food, art, and culture.

Her talk show "Getting Real With Pamela" is a purposeful show about passionate life journeys on www.evertalktv.com and is also available on Apple TV. Guests on the show range from entrepreneurs, artists, life coaches, and other driven professionals who share their struggles and successes in living a fulfilled life. Additionally, she is a writer, producer, and entrepreneur. Her most important role is to her family, being a loving and devoted mother to her most beloved son. Pamela strives to empower and encourage others to live their best, real authentic life!

CHAPTER 4

Crank Up Your Engine
by Karim Ellis

*T*he top was down on my Porsche convertible and music blared as I sped around taking care of errands. One more stop at the post office, and then I'd head back to my house for a relaxing afternoon in my backyard. As I hopped out of my car, set the alarm, and headed for the building, I noticed three kids around the age of ten wandering through the parking lot.

As I came out submersed in thoughts of what I needed to do, I looked up to see the three boys surrounding my car, admiring it. As I unlocked the car, one of them said, "Hey, mister, that's a nice car!"

"Thank you," I replied.

The young boy then asked, "How fast?"

I paused because I wasn't sure exactly what he meant. He asked again, "How fast?"

I turned to face them and replied, "What exactly are you asking, young man? Are you asking how fast the car can go? Or are you asking how fast I've driven it? Because the quality of your questions in life will always determine the quality of your results."

He paused for a second. I wasn't sure if he fully understood what I had just said. Before I could repeat the question, he boldly said,

"Well, both. How fast can the car go, and how fast have you driven it?"

"The fastest I've driven this car was 140 miles per hour." The kids' eyes swelled in amazement and their mouths dropped wide open.

"Wow! You drove it 140 miles per hour?" the young boy asked.

"Yes, I drove it 140 miles per hour. To answer your second question, the car can actually go as fast as…" Just before I got to finish my sentence, my conversation was abruptly interrupted by the slamming of a car door. A heavy-set lady with a look of disgust on her face yelled, "Why in the world would you do something so stupid and reckless as drive that pretty car 140 miles per hour? Better yet, why are you entertaining these kids with this nonsense?"

A silence descended over the group. I was shocked that a stranger would challenge my conversation this way. I looked the woman firmly in the eyes and began to explain my actions. Before I could get out a single word, she stormed off.

"Listen, the time I drove the car 140 miles per hour was around midnight and I was alone on a long stretch of highway, so I kicked the car into fifth gear and hit 140. There was no danger. Now, about the second question. The car is designed to hit speeds in excess of 180 miles per hour."

The boy who asked the question stood in amazement. I finished it off by saying, "Cincinnati, Ohio is full of 25 and 35 mile per hour streets. The car is designed to hit speeds in excess of 180 miles per hour. So, if I'm not careful, I could get comfortable driving 25 and 35 miles per hour.

"So, every once in a blue moon, I'll find an open stretch of road and crank this thing up as fast as I can." I could tell that my explanation hit home as the boy gave me a high five and we all parted ways.

My life has been filled with those 35-mile-per-hour roads always trying to stop me from reaching my full potential. Some limitations were self-imposed through failures and defeats. Some limitations were forced on me by family, friends, and even enemies.

Limitations are like speed limit signs. If you believe that the sign has governing power, you will never try to exceed or go beyond that.

Some of the limitations I've had to overcome are:

- Being a college dropout
- Being a person of color and the racism that goes with it
- Being out of shape; people thought I was lazy
- Low self-esteem

I believe that most people spend their life inside a bubble called a comfort zone. Most of us typically operate at speeds in which we are comfortably used to when it comes to chasing our goals and dreams.

Life's daily routines create the habit of performing at or below average when we have been uniquely designed, and have the ability, to do so much more. Which brings up a question: "What are you designed to do, and how fast are you designed to go?"

The world is full of people who are designed to go 180 miles per hour but spend most of their lives driving around on 25- and 35-mile-per-hour streets. They have been designed to win, but they drive to lose.

The Bible states that you have been created to be the head and not the tail. Whether you realize it or not, you're designed to be in first place, not last.

But you won't fully understand and operate in that mode until you figure out how fast you're designed to go. I believe that you can do more, be more, and have more.

It all boils down to you understanding what's under your hood. What are your gifts? What are your talents? What is your expertise?

What has the Almighty put inside you that lets you crank up your speed in your current season of success? Here's the bottom line: how fast are you designed to go?

For me, things didn't change until I realized I was "driving on the wrong roads." I started to surround myself strategically with people who had the lifestyle that I desired. This grew the belief inside myself that I could do it too. We spend a lot of time hanging around what we don't want, so I had to start hanging around with what I did want.

I hung around people who were successful regardless of their scholastic results. People of color who made it despite their birth heritage. People that gained control of their health and wellness. People that turned pennies into millions, and those that have high self-esteem. Those decisions helped me as I stepped out into two new areas: real estate and professional speaking.

I had worked a 9-to-5 job to pay the bills, then started a home-based toy business focused on selling vintage toys from the 80's, 90's, and 2000's. I used the side income from that business to stockpile money for investing purposes. When I was ready, I found an amazing mentor to help me use the money I had saved to flip properties. This eventually allowed me to create a debt-free lifestyle.

Once that happened, it was time to live my dream as a motivational/professional development speaker, and I love it. That brings me back to the beginning of the chapter and why I had to share with those boys that valuable seed. I had "slow down" signs placed in front of me most of my life, but not anymore. Now I control the speed. What about you? Isn't it time to get rid of the stop signs holding you back and drive the speed you are capable of driving?

Here are three simple ways to start increasing your speed:

#1: Who is your driving instructor?

When I was 16 years old, I told my parents I wanted my driver's license, so they sent me to driver's education class. I went through the in-class portion where I passed the written test. Then they put me in the car where I drove around for a week and a half with a driving instructor showing me what I needed to do to pass my driver's test and get my license. A license is your permission to drive.

So, who needs to be your driving instructor when it comes to increasing your speed in this season of your life? Who is the person who sits in the car with you and shows you how to manage and operate the unique gifts and talents the Almighty has put inside of you?

When I wanted to learn real estate, I found a real estate mentor who became my "driving instructor" for real estate. When I wanted to master speaking, Mr. Les Brown was my "driving instructor" for speaking, and still is. Those are two powerful individuals who have helped me get on the road to my goals and dreams.

So, who do you know right now who can help you get yours? Who do you need to specifically seek out to help you get out there on life's superhighway and crush it? Every successful person has someone they have studied or mentored with who has taken them to the next level.

#2: Where's your test ground?

I love Porsches. In fact, I'm a Porsche fanatic. I love looking at statistics on these cars. It is important to realize that Porsche doesn't snatch these statistics out of thin air. They don't make things up.

Before they sell a brand-new car to the consumer, they will take that car to an open track and test out the limitations of the car in different conditions. They'll crank the car up to 150 miles per hour on sleet, snow, high wind, rain, and gravel so they know what the car will do before selling it to the consumer.

Where's your test ground? Where's the place where you can go out to test and stretch what's inside of you? Where can you test not only what you're designed to do, but exceed the limitations of what you are capable of doing?

When I first started out in real estate, the way I tested myself was to hang with folks inside the local real estate investing club. That was my testing ground. That was my nesting ground. That's where I saw what I was designed to do.

As a speaker, I did the same thing. I joined my local Toastmasters, which is a speaker's club. Actually, I joined three Toastmasters clubs at the same time. I was president of two and vice-president of a third.

It wasn't because I was gung-ho about Toastmasters; my job was to get up in that arena and speak as many times as possible under different conditions, with different audiences.

I used stage props, live props, and spoke with no props. I even did presentations using my two Yorkies because I wanted to see exactly what my gifts and talent were capable of under controlled conditions.

What is your testing ground? Do you want to be an entrepreneur? A musician? A cook? To climb the corporate ladder? Cool. So, where is your testing ground – the place that allows you to test the very thing that the Almighty put inside you, where you can crank up your internal engine to hear what's under your hood? People get really good really fast when they play inside their testing ground.

#3: Who's on your racetrack?

Moment of truth: I am not the biggest NASCAR fan. Despite that, I have watched races before, and I'll tell you something. I've never seen NASCAR vehicles on the track mixed in with a moped, a Ford F-150 truck, a scooter, or someone on a bicycle or roller skates. You'll never see that in a NASCAR race. Why?

Because when you watch a NASCAR race, everything on the track looks the same. The cars may be different colors. They may have different logos, but they're all NASCAR-regulated cars. Getting on a racetrack and knowing you're racing against similar people and similar vehicles is a much more powerful experience.

When you're sitting at the starting line and they're counting down before the flag waves, you look to your right, you look to your left, and who do you see? Do you see people in pursuit of the same goal, using a similar vehicle as you? Because if not, chances are, you may be on the wrong racetrack in the wrong race.

When I look at my current racetrack, I see powerhouse individuals like Les Brown and The Message Midwife, Dr. Ona Brown. I see powerful motivational speakers like Dr. Stacie NC Grant, Dwight Pledger, and Johnny Wimbrey.

I see all these dynamic speakers because I want to become the sum total of the five people I hang with most. This is how I know I'm on the right track, pursuing the right goal.

As a speaker, I don't want to be on a racetrack with anyone average or mediocre. I want folks who are going to challenge me and push me to crank up to the level of speed I know I'm designed for, and not merely what I'm comfortable with. So, who is on your racetrack?

For you to go up, there are certain things you've got to be willing to give up. Please understand that what got you here is not what's going to take you there. To be super successful will require a different level of thinking and different actions from you. Different actions present different opportunities. Different opportunities create different results. What are the risks you're willing to take to discover your true speed and potential?

Just how fast are you designed to go?

Karim Ellis

Karim Ellis

Known as the "Message Motivator," Karim R. Ellis is a Dynamic Powerhouse Speaker with over 10 years of experience in speaking, training, coaching, and breakthrough success. As the author of the upcoming book, G.P.S. Your Success, Karim takes great pride in developing both leaders and champions. His messages and concepts help people to grow to the next level and beyond as he inspires an atmosphere of greatness in the lives he connects with.

Karim is also a member of the National Speakers Association, Past President with Toastmasters International, and is the owner of two successful businesses for 20 years.

As a member of the John Maxwell Team and as a Les Brown Platinum Speaker and protégé, Karim inspires and teaches Leadership/Professional Development principles to over 70 organizations a year.

When Karim delivers a message, he absolutely makes sure that the room "gets it." If you are ready for a fun, engaging, entertaining, and inspiring motivational speaker that will leave you amazed…Karim R. Ellis is definitely it!!!

www.karimellis.com
info@karimellis.com

CHAPTER 5

Honor Your Self-Care
by Patrick Tyrance, Jr., M.D.

O n Sunday, July 28, 2013, my father lay in his hospital bed – the same hospital where I once worked – with an IV carrying donated blood to his body, as his own body was unable to produce enough red blood cells to sustain him. A thin, fragile figure now replaced his once tall and proud muscular frame. Although it had been a few years since I worked there, individuals mistook him for me.

Despite the changes in his appearance, we still bore a similar resemblance. Although as a young boy I didn't like it when others mentioned our similarities, it didn't seem to bother me much as an adult, and even less so on this occasion.

He was lying in the hospital bed. My mom, sister, and a few family friends were outside his room talking, which gave us a few rare moments alone together.

I had been spending recent weeks working and traveling more than usual, unconsciously avoiding the fact that my father was dying. There would be mostly tough days sprinkled with a few good days between us. We exchanged a few words – mostly superficial talk, as we often did. Much of my childhood was spent revering and being intimidated by this man whom I believed to be superhuman.

However, at this time, he appeared mortal. I didn't know what to say to him – my idol, the one who so heavily influenced my mindset even as a young adult. Most of my athletic and academic pursuits were for him – to impress him, for him to be proud of me, and to hear him say "Good job," or "I love you." I heard it more as an adult and reveled in the confidence and security I felt when hearing it. He had softened quite noticeably in the past decade.

As he lay in the bed, I felt a deep connection and oneness with him as I had never felt before. It was both unnerving and peaceful at the same time. He was still, eyes closed, and speaking to me intermittently but all I could see was myself. Was I looking in a mirror? I saw a tired little boy who was taken by surprise – who found himself fighting for a life that was quickly coming to an end in a way he would not have predicted. It felt like a transference of sorts.

I wanted to lay next to him, snuggle with him and let him know how much I loved him and appreciated the way he had lived his life. He was far from perfect and provided many life lessons on what not to do. But, he provided for his family, did the best he could, instilled hope, and helped create in us a vision of a future brighter than the past we had known.

At this moment, I felt he desired to be seen and appreciated for the life he had lived. I was not able to muster the courage to let him know how courageously I thought he had lived his life. Instead, I just sat there and engaged him in topics of little importance. He wished me a happy birthday as I would be turning forty-five in a few days.

I smiled, thanked him, and said, "I love you," then leaned over and kissed him on the forehead before walking out of his room. My gut told me this would be the last time I'd see him alive. He had given his all to life and lived as best he knew how, but this life was quickly leaving him.

The following day, I would be traveling out of the country, and he would be heading back home to Charlotte, NC, to stay with my sister. We were all adamant about him returning to his home state and getting him back to the beach where he often vacationed along the southern Atlantic coast.

Friday, August 30, 2013, I was in rural Nebraska, seeing patients at a satellite clinic. It was the usual busy morning performing a few outpatient procedures in between seeing scheduled patients in the office. My father, anemic with the progression of his myeloma, was now too weak to make it to the beach.

To help recreate the experience in his mind, my mother and sister gave him a jar of sand and shells from the coast and recorded ocean sounds which played in the background during his frequent periods of rest. It offered him moments of relief to take his mind off the cancer.

My cell phone buzzed unexpectedly in my pocket. I saw it was my mother, excused myself from the patient's room, and told the staff that I needed a moment. Mom and I exchanged greetings. She told me Dad had received radiation to his spine to control his pain and that he wished to speak to me.

The multiple myeloma – a type of blood-borne cancer that produces an excessive amount of plasma cells (which normally produce antibodies) and crowds out the growth of other cells – left him anemic with a tendency to bleed and a weakened immune system. He was now completely paralyzed from the waist down as the cancer had spread to his spine and would require the assistance of a mechanical lift to assist with transfers and his physical therapy.

After a brief pause, a barely audible voice said, "Hey Tony (my dad's nickname for me). How are you doing, son?" Though very different, I still recognized it was my father's voice on the line. My eyes swelled with tears, and fighting back the desire to cry, I asked how he was doing. I listened as he told me he was feeling fine, loved me, and was proud of me. I responded with, "I love you, too," and "I'm hoping to get there to see you soon."

After hanging up, I sat in the bathroom as the pent-up tears burst from my eyes. I was full of emotion – anger and hurt. Upset with myself that I was not there for my father as I had hoped. Mad that I felt stuck taking care of patients for a hospital system that seemed to care more about its bottom line than those it employed.

My heart was hurting. I released a moan and wrapped myself in my arms to gain some relief. I still had patients to see. So, after a few minutes, I dried my eyes and cleared my nose to regain my composure as best I could. Looking back at our phone call and my father's knowledge of how I was choosing to respond to his illness by drowning myself in work, I believed it was his way of saying goodbye, knowing I was unlikely to see him again.

I was on-call with the ever-present anticipation of a call from the emergency department and having to go into the hospital. Just before midnight, I received two calls from the on-call emergency medicine physician regarding patients requiring admission and an orthopedic surgery evaluation.

Approximately three hours later, Labor Day, August 31, 2013, I received an early morning phone call from my mother. I could not make sense of the sound in the background and my pulse rate quickened as she screeched, "He stopped breathing! He stopped breathing!" Voices were now clamoring in the background. I responded, "Let him go, Mom… let him go! Whatever you do, do not let them place a breathing tube in his airway or try to resuscitate him. He's suffered enough."

He was listed as DNR/DNI – do not resuscitate, do not intubate – an important discussion we had as a family several months before.

However, I knew at the time my mother would be inclined to do everything possible to hold on to him and to keep him around.

My sister had left less than an hour before, after being with him for days at a time. I believe he knew his daughter was not present and used it as an opportunity to leave without burdening or traumatizing her. Even in his last moments, he was still looking out for and caring for his family the best he could.

I spoke with the physician who had entered the room and confirmed that my father had passed. After thanking him for his efforts and ending the call, I was filled with varied emotions – deep regret and sadness for not laying with my father in the hospital a month earlier; anger towards the hospital administration where I worked, who were less than understanding to my requests for time off in order to spend time with my father.

I was even upset with my father for leaving us so soon and not fighting harder. My heart became heavy and felt as though it had fallen deep into the pit of my stomach – a place that I didn't even know existed. I cried on the phone with my mother. I tried to console her mostly by listening to her, with a few comforting words of my own.

After the call ended, I phoned my boys to let them know their grandfather had just passed. I was able to reach Patrick III, my oldest, and spoke with him a short time. I also left a brief message with Jordan. It was now close to 3 a.m. when I tried to get some rest from the strain of the previous eighteen hours.

I awakened at 7 a.m. and went to the hospital to see the patients admitted the night before. They had been medically cleared for surgery in the early morning and were taken to the operating room. I had a brief conversation with the scrub nurse and circulator regarding the equipment necessary to complete the procedure.

I was still in a state of shock and numb to the idea that my father was no longer alive, and I was moments away from hiding in the busyness of surgery and caring for patients.

I did my best not to let my outward appearance reflect what was going on inside of me. Despite my best efforts, my facial expression must have been telling. As we continued preparing for surgery, the nurse stated that I appeared distracted and asked if everything was okay. I answered with a perfunctory, "Yes, I'm fine." I then stepped out of the operating room, made my way to the scrub sink, and began asking God for guidance, clarity, and decisiveness of thought and accuracy of hand as I had always done while scrubbing my hands prior to surgery.

These were routine surgeries that I had performed hundreds of times before. However, my direct request was much needed this time. My hand-washing routine was interrupted more than once by sobs and a realization that I'd never see my father alive again.

I questioned the value of what I was doing, whether or not I was making a real difference, and whether or not my efforts to develop a professional career were worth it. Why had I grown to dislike my job, feeling unfulfilled and defeated? Despite my emotional state, I was able to regain my composure, refocus and, uneventfully and successfully, complete both surgeries.

Between cases, I made my way to the emergency department to let the on-call emergency medicine physician know they would no longer have someone on call for orthopedics, and all potential admissions would need to be diverted to other hospitals. There was a brief exchange with the on-call emergency medicine physician and nurse house supervisor who initially denied my request. They then accepted as I explained my circumstance, and it became clear that I was not going to back down.

After I completed my last surgery, I assured the nursing staff that they could reach me directly on my cell if necessary. Then, later in the early evening, I drove home to catch a plane to Charlotte to be with my mother and sister and bury my father.

My phone calls to the hospital medical director were returned early the following day, offering condolences. I stated that I would be away for two weeks, and yet after one week, my phone was repeatedly ringing with messages asking for me to return.

This reinforced what I had previously felt. The hospital leadership and the culture it fostered did not support the mental and emotional health of its staff. It was secondary to profit.

I don't see the well-being of staff and profitability as separable; neither one can exist for long without the other. Inspiration and motivation cannot coexist in a group without "caring." An inspired, motivated staff will be more productive, more effective, and will offer more compassionate, heart-centered patient care that is also profitable for the hospital.

Their rationale for asking me to return only possessed the short sightedness of the profitability my services would bring to the hospital and revealed that they were losing money by my absence. It lacked the very benevolence of why I became a doctor in the first place.

Although angry to the idea of returning before planned, I justified my decision to return by telling myself it would be helpful for me to get back to work and return to my routine. However, I realized this would not be the case. My anger, hurt, sadness, and depression deepened, and I knew that true healing was not going to happen from this unhealthy environment. I needed out.

Within a week of returning to work after my father's death, I decided I would leave my position and only fulfill the six months remaining on my contract.

Our health care system more closely resembles a "sick care" system with little focus on the causes of illness and prevention. I was practicing in a hospital environment with well-intentioned individuals that functioned within a healthcare system that was dependent upon the sick. It was built on treating symptoms and did little to address the root cause of illness and disease.

All of these events led me to question what it was I was doing; to evaluate the impact I was having on my patients and the toll it was taking on me. I decided to take time off to find answers and take deliberate action toward living a healthier lifestyle.

What exactly would I be doing after leaving the hospital? I was unsure. My immediate plan was to complete the MBA degree I had placed on hold months before. I would also use the time to explore other buried interests, such as painting and music.

After being away from medicine for fifteen months, I returned to orthopedic surgery and joined a group practice. I found myself again in an environment centered around sickness, and I needed to align with a more holistic approach focused more on finding causes instead of treating effects. After six months, I left the group to open my own surgical practice.

I took time to travel, complete my business degree, attend personal development conferences, and study nutrition. I committed to a healthier lifestyle by cleaning up my diet, exercising greater self-discipline in my meditation practice, and moving close to the beach in southern Florida.

I now take a more holistic approach to treating my patients. In making my non-surgical recommendations, I am inclined to suggest meditation, breathing exercises, and various supplements in addition to the common modalities such as physical therapy and rest.

Regarding my health, I am more intentional in maintaining healthy boundaries that allow for self-care and maintenance. I am more aware of the company I keep and how I spend my time. I now understand it is not selfish, but okay to make me and my health a priority.

So, when asked, "Who cares for the caregiver in you?" the answer is you! You are primarily responsible for your own physical and mental health and wellness. We are all caregivers, and each of us is our primary caregiver.

Our environment matters – all of it, both internal and external. Our internal environment involves not only the food we eat and water we drink, but it is also the thoughts we entertain, the words we use, and actions we take (or don't take) that matter.

Our external environment includes how we spend our time and who we spend our time with. It either supports us in creating a healthy lifestyle or takes away from us being our best. All of this creates emotions inside us, along with a chemical response that is health-promoting or disease-promoting.

We have the ability to choose.

I also want to encourage you to remember that:

- The people closest to you matter. You do not know when they will be taken from you. Take every precious moment and show them how much you care.
- Your career is not who you are. Think of who will mourn you when your time is up.
- Your dream life is not always what you thought it would be. Take time to evaluate where you are and if your dream is still serving you.
- You get to decide what your dream is. Don't let others tell you how to live your life.

Thankfully, now I get to live my dream of providing healthcare in a way that prioritizes me and my patient's needs. My father's passing was the wake-up call I needed to change my life. I encourage you to look at your life and don't wait for something tragic to happen for you to live your dreams.

Patrick Tyrance, Jr., M.D.

Patrick Tyrance, Jr, MD.

Dr. Tyrance is a Harvard-trained physician and orthopedic surgeon with 15 plus years of experience. His orthopedic practice focuses on sports-related injuries, hip and knee replacement, and trauma. He takes an integrative approach, incorporating plant-based, holistic and non-operative solutions to patient care that considers the individual and their health from several vantage points – physically, mentally, relationally, and spiritually to maximize his patient's health and performance.

He received his bachelor's degree in Biology from the University of Nebraska–Lincoln where he was also a three-year starter and two-time Academic All-American on the Nebraska Cornhuskers football team. He earned his medical degree from Harvard Medical School and a degree in health policy from Harvard's Kennedy School of Government. He completed his orthopedic surgery training at Massachusetts General Hospital and the Harvard Combined Orthopedic Surgery Program and later earned an MBA in healthcare from The George Washington University. He is an active advisor for several successful start-up medical device enterprises and healthcare technology companies.

Instagram: Patrick.Tyrance
LinkedIn: LinkedIn.com/in/patricktyrance

CHAPTER 6

Push Through to Victory
by Danielle Rocco

*P*ounding footsteps snapped me back to the present. The man I called my husband was approaching. It was time to fulfill the duties of a loving, dedicated wife, mother, and business owner.

The clock in my office slowly chimed 3:00 p.m. and I was exhausted. I had been carrying the weight of years of unfulfilled dreams, self-loathing, boiling dissatisfaction, and disgust from neglecting my values and worth. That weight now drained me faster each day. I yearned to stop the thoughts that were overpowering me. I had to get out of that office, no matter how much guilt would hit me later.

In the 19 years of being the CEO of our family gymnastic business, I had always been there, never leaving early even once. For goodness' sake, on the way home from the hospital after all three of my children were born, I stopped by to make sure everything was running smoothly.

My brother and I ran that business like a fine-tuned machine. I opened the doors in the morning by 7:00 a.m. and closed them at 8:30 p.m. each night. My brother had the same dedication, and beyond that, we had a special spiritual connection.

When we were young, he would know when my heart was broken before I even walked through the door. I could never lie to him; he would look into my eyes and know exactly what I was thinking and feeling. God gave us each other, and together we could conquer anything. It was a blessing, as our father was mentally unstable and in a constant state of paranoia and hatred.

We kept each other strong through everything including our father praising us one moment and wanting us dead the next. My strong, humble brother had always protected me from our father and life, even when I didn't want his protection.

Together, my brother and I had taken our unique bond and created not just a business but a culture. We made sure that everyone who came through the doors felt loved and secure. People rarely noticed this silent energetic pull until they were not a part of it anymore. We would watch as students graduated, and year after year, returned to fill their internal bucket with the love that flowed so freely in that place.

I didn't want to go home, and yet I was so weak. My brother never questioned my intent when I left early. He looked at my pale face with concern, hugged me, and told me to call him later to check in.

The ride through the sleepy coastal town to the place I called home was only ten minutes. It was the same route I had driven for the past 19 years. Many days I had made that trip with no recollection of the drive. My mind would be far off, thinking of what I needed to do, what I would make for dinner, or filled with blank silence.

Through the window of my car, I could feel the warmth of the January sun. Feeling the sun beaming down on my cold, pale skin was a breath of fresh air. I remember thinking that maybe the sun appearing was a sign the winter wouldn't be dreadfully long and depressingly dark. A blanket of a light dusting of snow covered the ground, sending beams of light through the air and giving a majestic feel to my ride.

The next few minutes passed as if I was in a movie slowing down for the climax. I drove past the white farmhouse with the red metal roof as I unconsciously followed the road. As the car hugged the right turn, I couldn't ignore the powerful, uneasy feeling rising inside me. I wanted to get home; I needed to be home and fast.

The car made its way through the hypnotic scene with minimal effort from me. All I wanted was to curl up in my bed and not wake up. I had no idea what to do with the emotions and questions that arose in me that day. I was overwhelmed and confused. The pain that I felt inside was becoming unbearable, and I wanted out. Out of this life I had created. Out from under a domineering husband and father.

I was scared of the unknowns, but I was also scared of what my life would look like if I did nothing. I silently begged for an answer – for a way out of where I found myself.

All you have to do is ask, and you will receive it. Do not try to control or understand the answer. It will come, and what you do with it will lay the foundation for the next phase in life.

I felt myself relax into my seat. My head fell to the right, and my eyes became heavy. I only had a mile to go; I could make it. What other choice did I have? Was I going to pull over and rest that close to home? That made no sense. I told myself, "I need to keep my eyes open for one more minute," but I couldn't do it. Then the thought came, "I will close them for one second. I know the road well enough to do that…"

My Life Changed in a Moment

The next thing I knew, a brilliant, bright, and overpowering white light consumed everything around me. I could hear the branches hitting the side of my car. I didn't care. I felt a strong sense of peacefulness. One moment I was in what I can only assume as heaven; the next, my eyes flew open, and panic filled me.

There was white dust everywhere and a strange whining sound coming from the passenger seat. My body was limp as I dangled sideways, staying in my seat only from the tight restraint of my seatbelt. Had I been here minutes? Hours? Where was I, and what had happened? My heart raced, and panic flooded my body. I had to escape. The seatbelt was crushing my lungs as it protected me from falling into the passenger seat. My mind screamed, and my body stayed frozen; crippled from the pain. Softly a voice whispered, "You survived for a bigger purpose than what you have been living." Then with power and authority, "Now move!"

Gravity held the driver's side door closed. Attempt after attempt to open the door failed. My SUV was pinned sideways in a tree. I was weak and confused, so my strength did not come from my physical body. My movements were not my own. I gave one last push, the door flung open, and I slid to the ground under the spinning tires of the hovering SUV.

The New Me

After I was rescued, they found that I had spurring of the spine in my neck, a ruptured and bulging disk, nerve damage, a severe concussion, and brain damage. Life for the next two years was a blur. At first, I could not move. I could not drink or eat. I could not talk; the pain was all my body knew, and it paralyzed me. My life had changed; the life that had been silently killing me was over.

I spent those two years with one focus: surviving. I had wanted out of the life I had created; during those two years, I would have given anything to have it back.

Little did I know this was the beginning of me owning my life and recognizing my dreams.

The process was long. I first had to learn how to love myself, then love my life, and most importantly, kill my ego. Each one of these steps would be a new skill I would have to acquire. I had spent 38 years developing skills that led me further away from my true self and my dreams. Now I had to find my way back.

How do you love yourself when all you know is putting others' needs in front of yours? By first finding out who you are. How do you love a life that has no sign of you in it? By understanding your desires. How do you kill your ego? By realizing everything that does not bring you love is your ego running your life with fear.

I became humble in my pain, and my pain became my blessing. It forced me to focus on me, starting with my physical body. However, with each new doctor visit, I would hear the same useless information. The only difference would be in their approach: "Take these opioids for the rest of your life," or "I am sorry, there is nothing we can do for you," or I would get the judging stare that screamed "you are a liar and you're crazy!"

All they did was give me the fire to prove them wrong. I was given a second chance at life, and all the doctors' lack of knowledge was nothing in comparison to God's power to redeem my life.

Spending hours researching new and unconventional ways to handle pain slowly gave me a love for my life. I could see the blessings in my life, and I grew a voice. I couldn't physically put my desires aside to satisfy others, so I was forced to speak up and make decisions based on what was best for me.

This opened my eyes to a new way of thinking and acting toward myself. I was still loved, even when I wasn't fulfilling the needs of others. The story I told myself - that I would be alone, unloved, and not needed if I spoke up - was being proven wrong.

I understood that from each decision I had made in life, a new part of my story was born. I could also see that I was in control of how I responded to people or environments in my life. Deciding to make a shift was up to me – a shift that would bring value into my life and not just give life to others.

It is not my job to satisfy the needs of the people in my life. All I am responsible for is spreading my love. How people react is out of my control. When I release control, the universe always takes care of everything.

People that did not belong in my life, like my father, slowly disappeared. New people that I didn't know existed showed up. I found myself saying with complete joy, "I can't believe this opportunity came my way!" As I healed, so did my marriage. The accident was a wakeup call for both of us. Is it perfect? No, but now we focus on learning how to love each other better.

A Life Worth Living

Listening to God talk to my spirit kept me in truth. When my ego crept in and said, "Give up; this pain is too much to handle," my spirit whispered, "Your life is worth living; you will not take your own life. You will share your gift and change the lives of many." That truth slowly built my love for me. Each day I found the strength to stay alive. I didn't look at my physical and emotional progress by the day, but by the months that passed.

My dream is now simple: to love myself more each day and to find ways to show others how to do the same. It is not easy. I am still limited physically, but where there's a will, there's a way. This chapter is one of those ways.

The three things I want you to know most are:

- Not every tragic thing that happens in your life is bad. Many times, those hard places change our life for the better.
- It is good to get rid of the toxic people in your life that are weighing you down.
- Obstacles are a part of OWNING your dream. There is always a way around, over/under or through whatever you are up against.

My ego still creeps up in unexpected and sneaky ways. What I have learned with such deep driven passion is this: anything that causes you pain, fear, guilt, shame or tears is not your truth. It is your ego fighting to keep you stuck, overwhelmed, and unfulfilled – safe but not your true, powerful self. Recognize this, and you have the force to achieve anything. Ask for the truth, listen, and then act with the love, peace, joy, and grace that is in you. I guarantee it will be hard; you will feel weak and question yourself. However, no adventure is worth taking if it doesn't stretch you emotionally and physically.

This is your new journey, and you get to dictate and edit every part of it. Breathe life into your dreams and embrace the love you have in you.

My brother and I are both living our dreams. Our paths have taken us physically to different parts of the world, but I have learned that he no longer needs to protect me. He, too, is released because I have found my worth, my voice, and I am owning my dreams.

Danielle Rocco

Danielle Rocco

Danielle Rocco is a mother, wife, and lifelong entrepreneur. Growing up as a professional ballerina, Dani developed her commitment and dedication to everything that life has to offer. As an adult, her athletic skills transferred and assisted in her in becoming a successful business owner.

At the age of 18, she started working for her family's gymnastics school and took the company from bankruptcy to financial abundance. The school maxed out its student capacity very quickly. After 23 years of being the CEO, Dani left her family business to follow her passion as a life coach & relationship expert. She started working with CEOs, but soon realized her heart and mission was serving our Military and Veterans. She is now the author of Devoted to a Soldier & co-author with Dr. Ona Brown in Own Your Dreams, has an online academy Next Level of You, TV show host, documentary producer of Devoted to a Soldier, partner in the Join Our Table Movement, Contributing Partner/Official journalist of The Magazine, and speaker.

www.danirocco.com
www.devotedtoasoldier.com

CHAPTER 7

Leverage Your Gift
by *Jerome Maldonado*

*M*y life growing up was incredible – outside of the classroom. With a great, extended family, I grew up in an environment to envy. However, life in the classroom was an entirely different story. Challenged with undiagnosed dyslexia and the inability to properly comprehend dialect, school was difficult for me. My mother was awesome. She always believed in me, encouraged me, and sought out help and tutoring for me. She pushed me to work hard and never give up.

My reading and spelling disability affected my confidence, giving me a constant feeling of inferiority. To compensate for my frustration, I acted out. By the seventh grade, my aggressive conduct had me kicked out of nearly every Catholic school in Albuquerque, except one. The principal at that school took me in, sat me down, and took the time to treat me like a person instead of a lost animal; she worked with me. Most of all, she believed in me at the crucial adolescent year of eighth grade. I thank Sister Ada for her impact on my life's direction.

My connection with Sister Ada wasn't the only relationship that set my path. In reality, it was the love and belief from my very persistent and fearless mother that gave me strength and belief in myself. I knew by the time I was in high school that I was born to do something great with my life.

These feelings always motivated me to push forward. In high school, I would tell myself that I didn't care that I read or learned a bit slower than everyone else. I promised myself that I would do whatever it takes to be great, so I worked my butt off. That was my superpower.

I was never the smartest or most intelligent, but I would work my competition to exhaustion and then press forward – the same thing with school. I looked at school as if it was a competitor. I told myself that I would kick school in the behind and succeed or I would die trying. My mission worked! I still handle challenges today in the same manner. I don't focus on the challenge or the problem. I stay focused on a solution, and I never lose focus on my end goal.

Looking back on my upbringing, I believe that was what set me up for the success I've experienced. Although I struggled in school, my mind was creative, and I was good at thinking outside of the box.

Having to overcome a disability gave me a push of resilience to never give up and never give in to what people say or do. Being challenged in a negative way by teachers and adults who were supposed to be supportive role models thickened my skin to the elements of life.

While reading and writing gave me trouble, my ability to earn and manage money with the heart of an entrepreneur has been a part of my inner soul since I could remember. Working and making money has always excited me.

From the age of 11, I did everything, including smashing and recycling soda pop cans, mowing lawns, selling newspapers in downtown Albuquerque, and selling popcorn and cotton candy at the local minor league baseball team's stadium. I liked working and was not afraid of it.

In fact, the desire for more of what life had to offer was in my blood, oozing out of every pore in my body. The reward of having my own money to buy what I wanted was motivating. Purchasing my own motorcycle at the age of 11 with my hard-earned money was gratifying and rewarding. My attitude and drive gave me the ability to do well everywhere I went, including college, despite my learning difficulties.

My work ethic allowed me to move up in positions at the grocery store where I worked from 15 to 19 years old. I was so excited to have a real job pushing carts and bagging groceries. I worked like a crazy, mad man every day and always went above and beyond what was asked of me.

I also had an appreciation for the opportunity to learn. My drive earned me a management position at the age of 18. Being in management was exciting. However, I was soon faced with the politics of the older, veteran staff that didn't like my excellent work ethic and I hit a glass ceiling in pay. Desiring a bigger challenge, by the age of 19, I was ready to move on to greater things. After leaving that job, I vowed it would be the last time I worked for someone else because I could only earn what someone felt I was worth per hour.

My college studies were challenging and time-consuming and another reason that I decided to quit working a job. Working on the side tinting windows and installing car stereos allowed me to have flexible working hours.

I loved cars and still do, but what I learned is that I could earn larger profits in less time by working for myself. Nobody ever taught me that concept, but I soon saw how critical it was to having more freedom.

The summer after my junior year in college, I made plans to go to Mexico for a vacation. I watched as friends scrambled to borrow money or worked crazy hours to earn enough to go on the trip. Meanwhile, I ran a simple $20 ad in the Sunday journal to advertise window tinting. I obtained enough work from one ad to earn over $1,000 in less than one week working evenings during finals week. In the early nineties this was big money to a college student.

I quickly gained an appreciation for being self-employed. Delivering a valued service gave me a realization as a young adult that leveraging my time for larger profits is more advantageous than working for an hourly paycheck.

By the age of 20, I was introduced to a direct sales company. I thought I'd found heaven on Earth in the first 30 minutes of the job interview. I could earn money by selling great products. I could build a team of people who could do the same and make money off of what they sold. I was sold, hook, line, and sinker.

Although I loved the concept, I sucked at it for over two years. The road to success in direct sales is long and can be trying. My family and peers doubted me and hated the direction I chose, but I never gave up. That internal fight that I had gained as a kid battling dyslexia kept me mentally strong through thick and thin.

Traveling this great country from corner to corner, educating myself with sales, self-help, and marketing skills, I drove up my debt to over $100,000 and pressed myself to the point of incredible stress and fear. I was in trouble and wasn't sure how to get out of it.

I remember being in El Paso, Texas and feeling completely defeated. It was a Saturday night, and I walked to the closest church, kneeling in front of our Sacred Mother in front of the locked church and crying like a baby. I pleaded with God to "give me a bone." I told God that I had given this opportunity everything I had, and I admitted to mistakes I had made. I promised that I would never give up, but I needed help. I felt lost and defeated.

Nothing specific happened that night, but that moment was a turning point for my career.

Wanting to open a new market in Florida, my colleagues Rick and Derin, who I have a special love for as "brothers," suggested San Antonio instead. I remember the call from Derin as if it were yesterday. The February night in El Paso was cold and gloomy, with snow falling from the sky, which is very unusual for the Texas city. Derin was excited to work with me due to my performance with the company thus far. I mentioned that I was considering moving to Jacksonville, Florida, instead of San Antonio.

His voice came through from the other end calm, with confidence, and genuine feeling. He said, "If you don't come to San Antonio, it will be the worst decision you have ever made."

After considering his words, I decided to move to San Antonio with the condition that I would go only to kick ass and financially beat everyone in the office. I fulfilled that promise, receiving awards and dominating in both the San Antonio market and nationwide. I became one of the top 30 money earners in a company with over 300,000 distributors. I hadn't done well for a long time, but my persistence and faith drove my success.

In 1997, the you-know-what hit the fan, and the Federal Trade Commission shut the company down. Barbara Walters on 20/20 aired a story of the company as a money hungry, illegal pyramid scheme.

My parents called wondering what was happening, advising me to come home. I felt young and vulnerable but going home was the last option. I didn't want to feel as though I had failed. I had gone from $15,000-$20,000 per month to zero overnight. What else could I do?

Back in Albuquerque feeling like a failure, I enrolled back at the University of New Mexico to finish my education. With the entrepreneurial fire still burning deep in my soul, I decided to dabble with a lawn service company to make an extra $2,000 per month to invest in the stock market. Within the first two weeks, I could see that there was big money in landscaping, concrete, and construction.

I had the belief that if you don't educate yourself, you end up in construction. That was completely wrong. In less than a year, I built a seven-figure company. I used my direct sales knowledge and invested once again in schooling and seminars to learn the trade quickly, hired staff, and got to work. I created what is still a seven-figure company that has made millions of dollars.

What does one do when they start making real money? Invest it. In what? I decided to invest in real estate, not knowing that would be my claim to fame.

First, I purchased a single rental home, and then a single lot that I subdivided and turned into two lots, then three homes, then four, then a small retail center, and then another. Then I decided to get into single-family custom homes, which led to land development, and on to retail and commercial development, one small purchase to another, one investment to a larger investment.

After a 25-year roller coaster ride with many businesses and stresses later, here I sit with a portfolio of millions of dollars – not a bad run for a Spanish kid with dyslexia.

What's funny is that the money no longer drives me, nor the desire to succeed financially. What drives me now is 1) my family, that I love and adore, and 2) my desire to give back.

Success is a funny thing. We all deserve it and are worth it. It is the decisions we make and the direction we take that shapes our future. I never gave up on my dream for more. However, there were clear steps along the way that helped me progress that I want to share with you here:

- **Financial Lesson #1.** Have an entrepreneurial spirit. Very few of us came from easy roads and silver spoons. Apply yourself to whatever you do, whether it is a starting point or an ending point, and you will thrive. Give 110%, and your reward in life will pay you back in ways that are unfathomable.
- **Financial Lesson #2.** Have a dedicated work ethic. Always remember to give more of yourself than what is expected. Even when you feel underpaid, serve at 110%, and your reward will come.
- **Financial Lesson #3.** Leverage your time and resources. Remember to maximize financial value in exchange for your time. Create value and quality in your product or service for others, and they will pay!!!
- **Financial Lesson #4.** Deliver quality. This time in my life always reminds me to do two things: First, always to keep your faith. God will never let you fall. Second, never give up. When times seem hard, never quit. God will provide so long as you have faith.
- **Financial Lesson #5.** Be persistent. Persevere and be willing to adapt to change. Your continuous efforts and ability to adapt to changing circumstances will open doors to your success.
- **Financial Lesson #6.** Diversify. Realize what your purpose is and what your desires are by exercising your mind and allowing yourself to dream. Your mind will open to new methods and ideas to lead you toward your true purpose and desires.

Life is God's gift to each of us. Our gift back to God is what we do with this life that He gave us. Finding my true purpose in life through following my passion and believing I was worth it gave me the ability to own my dreams. When you own your dreams with action and faith, you will acquire anything you want in life. I am living proof, and you can be too!

If I had to sum up everything in a few sentences, it would be this:

> *Work hard. Always believe in yourself even when life and others don't. Know that God is no dummy. He put you here for a purpose, and He needs your talent, hidden or not, and never, never, never give up on yourself or a dream!*

I believe in you. Now it's time for you to learn how to believe in yourself, take control of your life, follow your passion, and continue to own your dreams.

Jerome Maldonado

Jerome Maldonado

Since 1993, Jerome Maldonado has been a self-employed entrepreneur, starting out in network marketing. His first introduction to real estate came from leasing offices for training and sub-leasing desks within his offices. This taught him how to create cash flow through real estate holdings.

In 1998, Jerome pioneered a new construction company, which he took to seven figures in less than one year. Understanding the concepts of leasing real estate, he purchased a multi-use commercial property to house his business. Jerome leased the remaining vacant real estate and had cash flow within 90 days.

This one commercial transaction gave traction and confidence to Jerome, and has allowed him to do millions of dollars in real estate transactions. In 2003, Jerome Maldonado founded J. Jacob Realty, LLC., which he is still currently active in. With his extensive resume, Jerome is currently producing training content and speaking on related real estate and business platforms. Jerome stated that 2018 was a year of diversification and business development and 2019 is a year of helping many business owners and real estate professionals do the same. He is excited to bring over 20 years of professional experience to the world in 2020!

www.jeromemaldonado.com

CHAPTER 8

Check Your Vision
by Mark Anthony King

S ometimes life is not fair. Unlike other teenagers my age, I was a mess. I had been emotionally abused since childhood by family and teachers and was morbidly obese by seventy pounds. Even though I was incredibly smart, I was labeled by the school system as autistic and unable to deal with life socially. I was put into a special class with the worst kids possible, which led to many more years of being bullied. All of this left me depressed.

To top it off, I had difficulty seeing clearly. Reading the chalkboard became increasingly hard, and I made it a point to sit as close to the front as possible.

One morning, my sit-and-squint-until-the-shapes-turn-into-letters strategy officially stopped working. I remember stretching my neck so close to the board, I felt like some sort of human/giraffe hybrid. Just as I was finally able to make out what my teacher wrote, she walked over to me and said she would be calling my mother after school to recommend that I see an optometrist and get my vision checked. Bless her heart.

I knew she meant well, and I knew how rare it was to find a teacher who cared so genuinely about her students, but at that moment, she was the lame teacher about to make me look like an even bigger nerd.

I remember sitting at home that night praying that she would forget to make the call. "Who am I kidding?" I said to myself, "She cares too much to forget." The phone rang a few minutes later, and I braced myself for the inevitable trip that was to come.

Sitting in the most uncomfortable brown plastic chair, in the notoriously cold optometry office, moments away from reading letters on a wall, I was fervently praying that I wouldn't need to wear glasses. Minutes slowly ticked by as I nervously waited for my name to be called so that I could take one of the few tests you absolutely cannot study for and definitely can't cheat on.

"That's it…" I thought to myself, "I'm squinting my way through this just like I squinted my way through social studies last year." That might not mean anything to you, but it was a huge victory for me, as I sat all the way in the back of that class. But I digress…

Eventually, my name was called, and I slowly made my way toward that creepy dark room in the back where I would take my test. The letters were already projected on the far side of the wall, and I immediately cursed the fact that I had thrown away so many carrots in my life because I could have definitely used their help right about then.

The optometrist greeted me as I sat down in the chair, and I realized I couldn't see squat, except for that massive E at the top of the list. I was definitely going to fail this test today and would most likely end up leaving with a pair of glasses.

That could have been great, but I didn't have the whole Clark Kent thing going for me at the time. There wasn't going to be an air of mystery where the girls are like, "Wow! You know, I bet he looks exactly like Superman when he takes his glasses off!"

I don't want to bore you with details, mostly because they're about me failing the test and being told that I would need glasses, followed by a solid ten minutes of me begging the optometrist to let me retake the test, and then begging my mother to please let me walk around blind. I'm telling you, I was negotiating like a trial lawyer defending his best friend from getting the death penalty. Sadly, the judge didn't rule in my favor that day.

When the optometrist handed me the glasses, I complained, I cursed, and I begged, but finally, I was able to calm down enough to put the glasses on. In that brief moment of literal and metaphorical clarity, I realized that I didn't know what I didn't know, and I couldn't see what I couldn't see.

When I put on those 1960s accountant glasses, I was able to see the world in a level of detail I didn't know existed. I could see tones, shades, hues, colors, and textures that weren't there before. They wouldn't have been there unless I had my vision checked.

I didn't see what was truly there. It's like I was viewing the world through eyes that weren't really mine. Not getting my vision checked had kept me from seeing what I was supposed to see in my life.

So, let me ask you: when is the last time you had your vision checked? In fact, if you took a vision test right now, how confident would you be in your ability to pass?

Before you answer that, let's establish some ground rules. First, you are allowed to wear your glasses or contacts if you wish. You can also stand as close to the letters as you want. So, now that we've established the rules, do you think you'd pass this test? You must be pretty confident, right? I mean, you have every single perceivable advantage at your fingertips, so passing should be virtually guaranteed. But what if you still failed this test?

I can't speak for you, but anybody in this situation would probably start coming up with a bunch of excuses, and rightfully so. It's the equivalent of failing a math test, even though you had a calculator and the answers right in front of you. In this particular situation, I would encourage you to come up with as many excuses as possible. In fact, make them until you completely run out of excuses, and you're only left with one thing: the truth.

You failed because even though you took the test, it wasn't grading your vision. I know it sounds crazy, but you've already come this far, so you might as well follow me a bit further.

It wasn't until I put on my glasses and changed my perspective that I was able to stop seeing things for how I assumed they were because I no longer had to guess. I no longer had to rely on the opinions or descriptions of others. That moment afforded me the blessing of being able to finally see things for myself.

That metaphor wasn't something that I would come to understand and appreciate until well over a decade after the fact. When I think back to that moment and the countless others that led up to it, I realize that it was one of the greatest gifts I had ever been given.

This metaphor is my gift to you.

When I was around ten years old, my father told me that if I went through life with no direction and with no vision, then I'd end up exactly where I set out to go… nowhere. So, from the get-go, the ten-year-old me understood two incredibly powerful and necessary things: the importance of having a vision and having a plan to make it a reality.

Having a vision gives your life a sense of meaning and a sense of purpose. My mentor, co-author, soul brother, and arguably the greatest motivational speaker of all time, Les Brown, once told me that (quoting William Barclay), "There are two great days in a person's life. The day we are born and the day we discover why."

The answer to why you were born is your vision. Having a vision for your life and something you feel deep in your spirit and knowing what you were placed on this Earth to accomplish, is one of the most powerful and beautiful things in the world.

Imagine the feeling of leaving this Earth without ever having answered your soul's calling. I don't want this for you. I don't want you to die with your magic still inside you.

The point of life is to live fully so that you may die with fulfillment. If you want this to happen, and if you want to live like few people have the courage to do, then you must have more than a vision. Seeing everything you've ever wanted off in the distance does nothing to ensure that you'll move an inch closer to it, let alone reach it. In this case, you need a plan that you follow because, as the saying goes, failing to plan is planning to fail.

Most people have something they want to accomplish and achieve. However, most people don't have a plan that they follow through to accomplish it, resulting in no action.

Incidentally, most people also never achieve their goals. I don't think this is a simple coincidence. Just like success has repeatable steps, so too does failure. Having a vision is great, but having a plan brings the vision out of your head and into the real world, turning what was once a thought into a possibility. Consistently following through with that plan will slowly but surely edge you closer toward your goal until the possibilities become your new reality.

Also, another part of checking your vision is freeing yourself and seeing the world as it is, and ultimately as you desire, by consistently doing the following three things every day:

1. Forgiveness. When it comes to forgiveness, I think Mark Twain said it best. "Forgiveness is the fragrance that the violet sheds on the heel that has crushed it." It is a beautiful sentiment; easier said than done.

My journey to forgiveness wasn't an easy one. If I had a chance to go back and do it over again, I would have forgiven sooner, and with reckless abandon, instead of picking and choosing what and who I would forgive over time.

Growing up poor and looking the way I did opened me up to being bullied by my family, my classmates, and my teachers. Their words and the way I let them affect me were things that I took with me everywhere. I carried them in my mind, and in turn, allowed them to weigh down my heart and spirit.

I dragged them everywhere like a ball and chain. In fact, the only thing that gave me some sort of control was not giving them the satisfaction of my forgiveness too soon. Waiting gave me a sense of power that, in hindsight, I know, was truly based on pain, resentment, and fear.

I learned a powerful lesson on the day that I chose to forgive without reservation. I learned that my life would never make sense, and my dreams would never come true as long as I kept viewing the world through eyes that only saw fear, resentment, and pain.

Take a look at your life, and the people who have shaped who you've become, for better or worse, and ask yourself two questions: "What am I holding onto that is holding me back?" and "Who am I blaming for it?"

Once you have figured that out, you can make the choice to forgive and walk through the process until you are free.

2. Focus. Imagine walking to your fridge, opening the door, reaching in, and grabbing a bright yellow lemon. Feel how cold and firm it is in your hand as you take a knife and slowly cut into it. Immediately that clean, bright, citrus aroma hits your nose and fills your lungs. Pick up one slice of the lemon, feel the juice dripping on your hand and then bite into the flesh.

Did your mouth water or pucker as you imagined this scene? If it did, that is the power of focus. Remember, the mind can't tell the difference between something you vividly imagine and something that happened. Anything you focus on, you will inevitably feel, whether you want to or not and whether it feels good or not. Thoughts have a habit of becoming things, and your only choice is to decide whether it's a nasty or good habit. It all depends on what you choose to focus on.

3. Daily Check-in. I remember when I first decided that I wanted to change my life. I was 18, in college pursuing a degree I hated, without a girlfriend, without a job, and I had recently decided that my circle of friends was pulling me further away from my core values. So I decided to distance myself from them, which meant that I was also alone. I thought about the things I needed to change, got super motivated, and gave it a solid effort for about two weeks before falling off the wagon.

Can you relate?

I continued this pattern for about a year before having my "aha" moment. I was binging on YouTube videos on a Saturday night when I came across a video that spoke about the importance of writing down your goals every day. I took it as a sign and decided to commit to doing that, starting the next day. The first list I wrote that Sunday morning was what I wanted for my life.

In a month, my life was totally different. I met a beautiful woman who taught me valuable lessons about myself, I discovered my passion for psychology, and I found a great new group of friends. Ultimately, those thirty days taught me that action without accountability leads to failure.

If writing down what you want is the first step, the second is observing the results your actions have been consistently producing, determining how effective your strategy has been at moving you closer toward what you want, and then adjusting accordingly. What specific results do you want to produce in your life, and what must you do to make it happen?

Checking your vision and the amazing ways it can create powerful shifts in your life is important. When it comes to achieving the things you want, the Internet and bookstores are full of powerful teachers, thinkers, and gurus who share their wisdom and insights. The great thought leaders of our time have their own ways of explaining the concepts, ideas, and strategies I'm writing about. Some of them have done this so eloquently, passionately, poetically, and with a level of esotericism that to this day, I still can't fully comprehend. All of the knowledge, concepts, personal stories, wisdom, lessons, and allegories have brought me to a simple conclusion: Check Your Vision.

What I truly want is for you to wake up each day with a burning sense of purpose, where you've got such a strong sense of passion that you don't have to psych yourself up to get out of bed because you can't wait to start the day and make it fully yours.

I want you to get to a point where you create your thoughts and emotions while dictating how you invest your time. I want for you to be connected to who you are at the deepest level, where you've moved past what's happened to you and embraced the beautiful lessons those moments taught you.

I also want you to be in awe of the beauty of life, the magic of existence, and how each lesson, good or bad, is shaping the incredible person you've become – the incredible person you can be proud of.

Good fortune favors the bold. Decide who you need to be and how you need to show up, and then boldly go after your dreams, making your life as magnificent as you dare.

Mark Anthony King

Mark Anthony King

Mark Anthony King is a Social and Emotional Intelligence Coach, Motivational Speaker, NLP Master Practitioner, Weight Loss Management Coach, Author, and Holistic Health Guru.

His unique process of systematic discomfort, practical psychology, and powerful mindset mastery tools allows individuals to release old stories, self-destructive patterns, and upgrade their belief systems. This system implemented during intense one-on-one sessions facilitates their ability to consciously create their ideal relationship, income, health, fitness level, and life.

An intense and energetic person, Mark's incredible love for people has allowed him the privilege of coaching hundreds of people from all nationalities, age groups, and all walks of life. His skills include helping couples to reignite that spark again, showing an entrepreneur how to fully claim their role as a leader, curing lifelong phobias, transforming a client's body or helping a suicidal individual rediscover the beauty, level of forgiveness, and strength that resides within them. A self-proclaimed "positive perfectionist," Mark strives for mastery in every aspect of his life, and his mission is to help everyone he works with tap into something he calls their "infinite potential."

www.LifeMasteryStrategist.com

CHAPTER 9

Take Calculated Risks
by Darwin Liu

*T*he birds were out and about, singing their daily melody in perfect cadence. The flawlessly orchestrated song and dance would have brought joy to any lucky bystander – anyone, that is, except me.

I was still under the covers when the birds started their songs. The room was pitch black, gloomy, and bare – a true reflection of my life. My dreams were all but shattered. I gave my heart and soul for the past two years with nothing to show for it. My parents were embarrassed; my friends thought I was a loser and looking in the mirror brought hate and self-loathing.

As usual, the birds slowly migrated in search of a more welcoming audience. My brain wandered, and I started to lose myself in my thoughts. My eyelids felt heavy as reality slowly faded…

A bright red Ferrari 458 sat in my driveway.
Black 22" rims, low to the ground, and an engine
that purred every time you revved the pedal – I
had hit the jackpot.
I was elated. I was more than that; I was stoked.
Why wouldn't I be? I had won at the game of life.
I proved to all the doubters that I wasn't an idiot,

*to my ex-girlfriend that I wasn't a loser, and to the
world that I wasn't a failure.
I pressed the "unlock" button on my remote
starter and waited for the gullwing doors to open
slowly. Nothing happened. I pushed it again, and
again, and again...*

A Gambler's Reality

The buzzing from my cellphone caused me to jump up from my bed. My imaginary utopia shattered, I peeked through the spiderweb of cracks and saw the familiar, "Do Not Pick Up, Debt Collector," on my screen. With a heavy sigh, I dropped the phone and crawled back into the safety of my bed.

The number 458 wasn't the model of my Ferrari; it was my credit score. I accumulated over $30,000 on my credit cards and hadn't paid a single penny in the last five months. My life was in a downward spiral, and it was no one's fault but mine.

I've always been a gambler. It's in my blood. The dopamine rush I get from taking risks is like a straight hit of crack cocaine. I gambled any chance I could get and, more often than not, I won.

This time was different.

I didn't spin the wheel, push my stack on black, and lose it all. I didn't flip a 10 and bust on 22 in blackjack. This wasn't the game of poker, and I didn't go all-in on a bluff. This was the game of life.

When you gamble in the real world, there are real consequences. I risked my future, my friends, and my reputation – and I lost it all.

Growing Up Poor

It was 1993, Bill Clinton had just become the President, and public sentiment was high. The economy was booming, job creation was at a record pace, and American citizens had more discretionary income than ever.

80

Businessmen and women were hustling and bustling to their high paying jobs. The smell of new construction was everywhere, and there was a new BMW on every corner.

Somehow, the wealth that every other American accumulated flew right by my family.

My mother coordinated folders by date, color, and department for under $6/hour. My father cooked crab rangoon for 12 hours a day. Instead of leaving with a retirement plan, he left with a failed kidney. With money being so tight, we didn't have much left over for food. Shopping at the grocery store, I always thought every other parent loved their kids more.

High school was rough.

I rotated between a pair of jeans that looked as if they went to war and barely survived. The thighs were faded from the original blue to a weird yellow hue. The knees were ripped and measured the size of a tennis ball. In some areas, the material was stretched so thin that you could see my skin. In the winter, the cold wind would slice through my knees and leave them numb. By the time I reached school, my socks were soaking wet. The physical discomfort was nothing compared to what I was going through mentally.

Thoughts of not feeling loved, being hated, and/or being different ran through my mind continuously.

The brevity of our situation was always on full display and, as a kid, you don't truly understand any of this. I hated my parents for being "cheap" and the phrase, "We can't afford it," was constantly used in our household. It was normal to wake up at 2:00 a.m. to broken dishes, shouting matches, and bouts of crying.

One day, I couldn't bottle up my emotions anymore and decided to confront my mother. I headed toward my mother's room and saw the light through the slit of her door. The familiar churning through her closed doors got louder as I slowly entered, uninvited.

At that moment, I finally understood what my parents sacrificed to raise us.

The churning noise came from the rotary sewing machine as my mother methodically pushed her underwear through the needles. She finished the patch and gently placed it on the already finished pile of clothes.

Calmly, she looked at me and said, "Darwin, it's a school night; why are you up?"

"Nothing, mother, I'll see you tomorrow."

With a look of unconditional love, she said, "Get some rest, I'll cook you breakfast before I go to work tomorrow."

My life was changed.

My mother worked extremely hard and never purchased anything for herself. Any additional dollar she could save went to raising us and giving us a better life. All her clothing had been patched up to the point of being barely recognizable.

Money wasn't the source of all evil; the lack of money was. The lack of money was the reason why my parents would fight over bills. Not having money was the source of my exile and ridicule at school. I finally realized that everything wrong in my life came from our family not having any money.

At that very moment, I knew I needed to get rich.

Failing

In the summer of 2008, I graduated from college. Instead of getting a job, I took the biggest gamble of all and placed my life in Google's hands.

I turned on my computer, opened up Internet Explorer, and googled, "How to get rich online?"

When reading rags-to-riches stories, there is a common denominator to all of them – they're all self-taught. I was never good at school, but I loved learning on my own. In any endeavor I take, I follow the same steps. Learn from the past, apply lessons, then make it your own.

I worked on my business for seventy hours a week and lost contact with the outside world. Not knowing a single thing about marketing, I watched videos and read tutorials. I applied what I had learned and asked questions about things I didn't understand. I continued this process until I became technically adept at web development, design, and online marketing.

Affiliate marketers were making $50,000 a day, and I wanted a piece of it.

To get traffic to my websites, I paid for ads through Google. For every $1 I made, I paid $3 in advertising fees. No matter what I tried, I couldn't turn a profit. Despair slowly crept up as my credit card bill got bigger and the bank account got smaller. Instead of the $50,000 a day in profit, I ended up owing $30,000 with no way of paying.

The dinner conversations slowly changed from Ferraris to my parents' embarrassment of me. All their friends' children had respectable careers, while I still lived in their basement. My parents looked at me with disdain, and my friends made jokes about me behind my back. Going to social outings usually meant ridicule and questions like, "So Darwin, are you rich yet?" I felt worthless, and rightly so.

The biggest issue in my failure wasn't the inability to pay my debts, it was admitting that I was wrong. Everyone was waiting for me to fail, and my applying for a job was validation. To everyone around me and myself included, failing was the end of the road.

Ready for the onslaught of "I told you so's," I applied and was immediately accepted for an entry-level position at a marketing agency.

Finally Becoming an Entrepreneur

Somehow, everything clicked after I admitted failure. I realized that all entrepreneurs fail, it's what we do afterward that separates the winners from losers. Most people quit after their first failure and never try again. Instead of their true potential, they end up doing something they hate. I finally understood that failing is part of the game, and I will fail many more times in my life.

Getting a job wasn't the end, but a means to an end. My job paid my debts and allowed me to chase my dreams. At heart, I was still an entrepreneur and was eventually going to go out and do it all again. I wasn't an entrepreneur in my job, but I was still going to be entrepreneurial in all my efforts.

Official work hours started from 9 a.m. and ended at 4 p.m. I was usually the first one in and the last one out. I went to work during holidays, weekends, and snowstorms. Our biggest client days often landed on my birthday, and I worked on that day too.

Although I was at the bottom of the totem pole, I had more experience than most managers at the company. While most people went home and relaxed, I was learning and building on my knowledge. With everything I did, I was able to help our clients make more money and, in turn, make our company more money.

My work ethics and knowledge skyrocketed me to the top. When clients needed things done over the weekend, I would be there for them. When the company required last-minute presentations, I stepped up to the plate. "No" wasn't in my vocabulary, and I became the pinch hitter. My personal brand was growing with our clients, within the company, and within our industry.

I was promoted every single year and ended up running strategy for our largest accounts. My parents were proud of me and started bringing me up in conversations again. I was making over six figures, my credit card debt was paid off, I drove a BMW, and life was good. What more could I have asked for?

Chasing Dreams

I was comfortable. Comfortability is carbon monoxide disguised, and I inhaled it for two years. Everything seemed fine from the outside, but I was becoming complacent and slowly being poisoned.

When I began my entrepreneurial journey six years ago, I did it for my family. As my journey progressed, it slowly became much more – it became a part of me. Chasing dreams, living your best life, and risking everything were ideas I represented. To the people I touched, I represented hope. Through me, they were able to see a better future for themselves. Through me, living their best life wasn't just a fantasy; it became a reality.

If I didn't finish what I started six years ago, I would be letting myself and everyone around me down. Most importantly, everything I represent would mean absolutely nothing, so I made a change.

Mother: "Did you lose your mind? Why did you just quit your job? You failed the first time; what makes you think it won't happen again? Think about what everyone will say. You're going to look stupid again."

Everyone around me thought I was insane and stupid. I've always been a dream chaser, and I'd rather live life knowing I tried and failed than to live life with regret. Everyone was telling me that it was a dumb idea. On top of that, the inner voice in my head was also telling me not to go for it.

In the summer of 2017, I quit my job and started a marketing agency. My agency provides digital marketing focused specifically on eCommerce.

We started with three people working in my condo living room. Having a good amount of savings but no income, it was still a risky move. There was some money coming in, but we were by no means a real company.

I didn't know a single thing about running a legit company, but like before, I hit the books. Applying what I learned, we formed partnerships to help us sell our services. We created internal systems, processes, and goals for all of our employees.

We're doing well, and if I didn't quit my job, then none of this would have come into fruition. Within the first year, we reached seven figures. We're now at fifteen employees and growing exponentially. I currently run multiple companies, and the rest is history.

No Risk, No 'Rari

Nine years ago, the birds were a constant reminder of my failed attempt at entrepreneurship. Today, the birds wake me up to a beautiful, bright, and happy life. Today, my cold, basement room doesn't seem so "cold" anymore. It was where I cemented my values and became an adult. It was where I started on a journey that changed my life.

If you played poker, you would know that you can't win every hand. The players who win the most are the ones who play consistently and grow. Back then, I thought I only had one hand. Little did I know that failure is part of the process, and the more I played, the more chances I had at winning.

TAKE CALCULATED RISKS

Many of us think we don't get to choose the outcome of our lives, but we do. I could live a life chosen for me or I could live a life chosen by me. I could have lived the life expected by my parents. I could have landed a nice stable career, but I didn't. I chose to go all-in for a chance at a life everyone dreams of. Growth comes with the willingness to risk your reputation, money, and permanency. Without immense risk, none of this would have come about. My parents' new house, my cars, and my businesses are a direct result and in proportion to the amount of risk I took.

Nine years ago, all I had were dreams. Today, all my dreams have become a reality and yes, I did get the 'Rari. When I went to the Ferrari dealership and picked out my car, it was liberating and validated all my goals, thoughts, and dreams. The car itself is an object, but being able to accomplish what I set out to do left me with a feeling like I was walking on air. Not only that, everyone around me now has hope that they're not stuck in their current path.

I want to leave you with three precepts to live by that changed my life:

- Failure is a part of success. Many times, you learn more from your mistakes than anything else.
- Hard work is an entrepreneur's best friend. It attracts success to you.
- You must be willing to learn your way to the top.

An entrepreneur's journey is often a lonely one. You will be misunderstood, but never let that stop you. Once you reach your goal, it will be worth the price you paid. For me, it was sitting in my 'Rari. What is yours? Keep that picture in your mind and work until it becomes a reality!

Darwin Liu

Darwin Liu

Darwin Liu is the CEO and founder of X Agency, a digital marketing firm specializing in ecommerce. After graduating college in 2008, Darwin googled, "How to get rich online," and discovered online marketing.

After many failures, he found an entry level job at a digital marketing agency. For the next six years, he grinded his way to the top and grew his own personal brand. When he left, he founded X Agency and within the first year, grew it to seven figures. Growing by leaps and bounds, he's ventured off into other forays such as Americanbully.com and many other investments.

www.xagency.com
www.darwinliu.com

CHAPTER 10

Say Yes to a Bigger Life
by Carol Feeley

I loved the sound of autumn leaves crackling as I stomped through them on the way to school. The neighborhood was filled with kids my age, and we would create games like acorn fights to play in our front yard. Some of my best memories were from my neighborhood in the early 1960's. Those were innocent times.

A change came in second grade. If I had been graded on my kickball capabilities, I would have earned an "A," but the playground where I had built my confidence wasn't where I had difficulty. I had a hard time concentrating inside the classroom and was easily distracted. I was never diagnosed with any problems of being hyperactive, but the educational system wasn't what it is today. Fortunately, it has improved greatly. Sitting still was hard for me; I became easily bored.

The school decided to solve this problem by putting me in what I call a "special room" with five other students who were also struggling in school. The room was unpleasant, with no pictures on the walls and seats that were oversized for our small bodies. Going back and forth between classes, I couldn't understand why I had to be separated from my friends.

That experience created an uncomfortable feeling of exclusion, like I was different. It was as if I no longer belonged. Looking back, I realize that I yearned to be closely connected with my classmates that I was separated from. While the school thought they were helping me, it took me on a downward spiral. I was locked up emotionally in that room for years, enslaved by my thinking that I was less than who I truly was.

My inner struggle led to thoughts of feeling unworthy. As a young child, I was very impressionable. My thoughts seemed like a broken record that would whisper lies, but I didn't realize that they were lies; I took them as truth. Phrases like, "I am not smart enough," or "people don't like me." In my early twenties, I took a self-destructive path, drinking to ease my pain of having a poor self-image, which became progressively worse.

I was invited to attend church by my friend Gloria. Through the church, I was introduced to great people who helped clean me up while I started taking responsibility for my actions. I stopped drinking and began a self-discovery journey to find out who I was and who I was not.

People showered me with love, and I felt like I mattered. My church was an integral part of my recovery process. Later, I learned to love myself and healing took place. To pay the love forward, I began to lead a women's Bible study. I related to some of the deep issues the women had, and together we bore each other's burdens. Everyone was flourishing as we all grew together.

I didn't have a great start, but it doesn't matter where you start. The thing that matters is that you start – and starting always begins with a "Yes."

Like Gloria, there have been numerous friends guiding me along my journey of life. One friend in particular stands out. About six years ago, the phone rang and it was my friend Nancy. She was eager to tell me about joining Toastmasters, which is an organization that improves your communication skills.

Nancy urged me to come to the next meeting, which was during my work time, so I told her I couldn't make it. Nancy was relentless, calling me two more times to attend. On her last call to me, her voice had a tremendous sense of urgency to join her at the meeting. At this point, I was so intrigued by her persistence that I asked my director for the time off to go with her to a meeting.

When I walked into the meeting that day, I met a friendly, energetic, supportive, and fun group of people. They were laughing and helping each other become better communicators. I was reminded of the neighborhood friendships I had so many years ago, and I joined their group. Somehow, I knew this would be a great "Yes." Joining was part of God's plan.

I consistently attended Toastmasters every week. In the book, The Slight Edge by Jeff Olson, the author shows how implementing simple daily actions consistently can transform your life. For me, consistent action of preparing and practicing speeches translated into a love for speaking.

When I held that microphone for the first time, I had a shaky voice and sweaty palms. Even with all of my fears, I did it. I enjoyed that speech more than I could ever express. I received thunderous applause, which resulted in my receiving the best speaker award. That simple recognition of a job well done kept me speaking. Seven years later, I am still speaking. In that speech, I said, "I was in the right place at the right time." I had no idea how that "Yes" was going to change the direction of my life.

The speeches I wrote and gave over the next year helped me say "Yes" to the next call. It came through my church: a mission to Kenya.

I had heard that call over and over throughout the years. I'd always felt an urge to go but was too afraid to say "Yes." This time, the call was different – or I was different. I felt a tug on my heart to go.

I remember that day so clearly at church. They showed a video about the trip and a strong emotion rose up in me when I saw the children who would be affected by my going. I decided to take all of my fears - the fear of flying, the fear of going on the mission trip - and say "Yes" to the call.

To go, I had to raise $6,000. I didn't know how I was going to accomplish it, but what I did know was I had the desire to go. Somehow, I was going to make it happen. I became braver than I ever had in my life. I learned to ask for donations. I learned to receive them. All of it took me out of my comfort zone.

The donations were coming in from unexpected places. God had a big sign that said, "Carol's going to Kenya."

While finding the funds, I had my doubters who said I wouldn't raise the money. It didn't matter what they were saying. I had a determination inside me that I never had before. I wouldn't give up until I raised it. At one point, I walked into Bible study and walked out with $650 for my trip.

People were doing garage sales and other fundraisers for me. The growth time for me was incredible as I believed in my goal and took action. The funds came in with the help of 34 amazing supporters who believed in me. I said "Yes" to the biggest adventure I ever had, despite all of my fears.

Four flights and 22 hours later, I mastered my fear of flying. Big tears of joy came down my face as we were minutes from our arrival. Then the stewardess said, "We are about to land in Nairobi, Kenya." It was a dream come true.

When you decide to say "Yes" to a bigger life, it doesn't mean it's going to be easy. Sometimes it's a fight, but when you are laser-focused with the right mindset, you can move mountains. There was a new strength inside me that took over my life, in a good way. I attribute much of my courage to the people that I surrounded myself with.

My passion for going to Kenya could have been destroyed by the self-doubt that I had for so many years. Saying "Yes" to Kenya and to a bigger life allowed me to experience things I would have never experienced. Moving the mountain in your life takes an unwavering passion for winning. When you have a strong enough reason, and you are clear on what you want, you will overcome the many obstacles that are sure to arise. You will keep fighting to take new ground when your desire becomes bigger than the hurdle you have to get over.

So, how can you keep your self-doubt from affecting you? Belonging to a tribe of people who believe in you is a vital part of your success. We are not created to be an island; we were created to be in fellowship. Toastmasters not only allowed me to say "Yes" to a bigger life, but it also introduced me to a wonderful tribe of lifelong friends. From my neighbor to everything in between, growth comes from aligning yourself with a good, solid tribe of people.

Jim Rohn said, "You are the average of the five people you spend the most time with." Who are you around? Do they have the same values as you? Do they encourage you to stretch yourself? If not, I would suggest finding a new group. Get a tribe of people around you who push you to greatness and will hold you accountable. When you are around winners, you will become a winner. Saying "Yes" to a bigger life helps you, and it affects everyone around you.

I never in my wildest dreams believed I would have the honor of writing a chapter in Dr. Ona Brown's book. When I was first approached about being a part of this project, my first thought was, "Is my story good enough or relevant…would it bring value to the reader?" I had learned to take control of my thoughts, and I accepted the honor of being a part of this project. I wasn't going to let my thoughts stop me any longer. When you say "Yes" to your life, you can do more than you think you can. Taking a risk in life is an adventure, and that is the only way to live.

Once you get started, saying "Yes" to life starts to become a way of life. Doubts will come, but as Dr. Martin Luther King Jr. said, "Faith is taking the first step even when you don't see the whole staircase." Those steps are the "Yesses" you make in life.

Lastly, it's those hard places where you find new strength. Welcome the hard places – they are where the growth lies. Take ownership of your dreams. Do you know what you need to say "Yes" to in your life? Most of us do. Embrace your inner strength and trust yourself. I have no doubt once you decide to move into action it will create a life you never thought possible.

Saying "Yes" on the journey at times can be hard but really worth it. That is the beauty of growth. I know you want to evolve, or you would not be reading this book. Is there something in your way that is stopping you? I want to encourage you to say "Yes" even when it hurts.

That "special room" that I had spent time in as a child haunted me for years. What is your room? What is holding you back from your greatness? If you are stuck in a room that you can't seem to find a way out of, take the following steps:

- Surround yourself with a tribe of people that will inspire you to take that step.
- Push yourself and take risks. Get a little uncomfortable. Like one of my mentors says, "Get a little dirty."
- Welcome the hard places where growth lies.

- Embrace your inner strength and trust yourself.
- Take action.

When you take these steps and find yourself on the other side of fear, you will feel so liberated. You will ask yourself, "What took me so long?" Once you start, the momentum builds. Allowing "Yes" to become your favorite word will be your fuel to get you to the next decision.

Take ownership of your dreams and you will create a life you never thought possible. If I can leave that room of labels and limitations behind and conquer my fear, so can you. Take the first step and say "Yes" to your dreams!

Carol Feeley

Carol Feeley

For over 15 years, Carol Feeley has implemented personal growth strategies to help transform her life and others. Southern California has been her home, and she loves to travel and has traveled as far as Kenya to spread her work in health.

For 43 years, Carol has been married to her husband, Jim. The secret to their longevity is patience, laughter, and letting her husband do the cooking. She has two beautiful daughters and is Grammie to Hannah Grace, plus she adores her son-in-laws, Jason and David.

Carol worked for many years as an energetic music & movement teacher as well as a storyteller to Pre-K children. With her storytelling skills and her love for empowering people, she is now a transformational coach and speaker. She inspires her audience with strategies to create a healthy mindset, a fit body, and a pleasant life.

Carol Feeley will inspire you to walk in your true individual path so you can "OWN your Dreams" and say "Yes" to a Bigger Life. Do you dream of having more focus and being more consistent with health and mental clarity? She will show you how to create habits that will benefit your health, mood, and overall life.

empowermentcoachcarol@gmail.com

CHAPTER 11

Find Your Inner Joy
by Alina Ugas

Ten years ago, on a beautiful sunny California spring day, I waited patiently in the long line at my favorite coffee shop, I noticed a tall, light-skinned, well-built gentleman who wore glasses and was bald. What caught my attention was his physique. After having worked in the medical field for 34 years, I notice things about people, especially their physical aspects. The shape of his head told me he was a preemie or was born underweight.

The next thing I noticed was what he was wearing; I thought to myself, "Why would anyone wear corduroy pants in this weather?" Just looking at him made me feel hot.

The gentleman noticed me staring at him. He turned around and looked down at me, "I can feel your piercing look penetrating my buttocks."

He seemed a little sure of himself, so I replied, "You need to get over yourself."

As fate would have it, that day was the start of a ten-year friendship and the true start to my emotional healing from a lifetime of trauma.

My life-altering experiences began in 1971 at the age of nine, in Havana, Cuba. In the early morning, my mother took my siblings and me on a spontaneous 12-hour train ride north from the province of Santiago to Havana. I was excited to be on the train because it was the first time I had ever left our province or that part of the island.

During the train ride, I stared at the cows, fruit trees, and mountains that I had never seen before. As much as I enjoyed this adventure, I still didn't want to be away from home.

Before the train ride, I overheard my mother say we were spending a few days in Havana. For some strange reason, she didn't allow us to take our dolls, toys, clothes, pictures, or any of our belongings – or say goodbye to our friends or family. That led me to believe that we would be home in a few days, making the trip more tolerable.

My mother's childhood friend met us in Havana and took us to the airport; the last place I expected to be. That's when I learned we were traveling to America to join our father. Suddenly, we went from a simple 12-hour train ride to leaving everything and everyone I knew and loved back home. I went numb from the overwhelming feelings that struck me. Then all hell broke loose.

Before we boarded the plane, my mother took her four children into the bathroom. She pinned a religious medallion to my undershirt beneath the blue, frilly dress she had made for me. She prayed to St. Barbara for our safety and believed it would protect me.

My mother always dressed me like a Cuban princess. She worried about what people would say about me and how she would be judged as a mother. Other people's opinions were everything to her. I remember when my mother looked into my eyes and told me if airport security found the medallion, it could be used against us. She did the same for each of my siblings. I was terrified of betraying the entire family if mine was found.

The immigration process was next, and the nightmare began. It was a white building with nothing on the walls; it felt sterile as if I were in a hospital. The air was humid and uncomfortable with so many people crammed into one area.

They called my family and put us in a big room with six men in military uniforms and rifles informing us to undress to make sure we were not carrying any contraband outside the country. I was nine years old and didn't understand what was happening. I was scared, powerless, and uncomfortable because I was the first person in my family who had to undress.

One man ordered me to take off my dress, and in tears, I pulled my dress down to my knees, leaving me with only a T-shirt and panties on. The solider then looked at me from the front and the back. I felt ashamed, belittled, and degraded. I had never undressed in front of any man before, not even my father. Fortunately, they did not touch me. I could not wait for this horrible experience to be over.

After they were finished with me, I watched my siblings and my mother go through the same inspection. This experience would be the first of many traumas I would endure.

As my body shook with fear, I walked toward the plane as if I were walking to my death. I was sad, confused, and angry. My mind spun from the shock that I would never be returning home.

"Why are we doing this?" I shouted as we walked toward the big metal tube with the letters "AA" on its tail. I had never even seen an airplane before. I thought the plane would travel on the ground. I didn't realize it was going to take off and fly through the air. What does a kid from a small town in southern Cuba know?

At the top of the steps, I looked back toward the airport and the country I would not see again for another 47 years. Reluctantly, I boarded this machine that would take me to a new land. At that time, my mind didn't know how to digest everything.

I thought to myself, "How can my life change so quickly?" I asked my mom, "Why do we have to leave?" Everything was new and seemed surreal. I have no doubt the majority of my fears in life developed in those fleeting moments – my fear of risk, heights, being assertive, the unknown, and more that would show up later in my adult life.

I remember how we left everything and everyone behind, including my mother's parents. She knew she would never be able to hug her mother, dad, or siblings again because of her choice to follow my father's dream. My mother's family was part of the Communist regime, and the government made it very clear that if she left the country, they would have nothing to do with her. Her family would disown her for her decision.

I sat in my seat as the plane shook, and the engines roared and lifted off the ground. I looked out the window and saw Cuba shrink as we went higher into the sky. I saw my past life shrinking and my unknown future expanding as I tried to make sense of it all.

We arrived in Mexico City a few hours later. We were in a one-bedroom apartment for the next six months. The language was similar, although different, and the food was disgusting. Who would wrap a bunch of food into a tortilla?

Fortunately, we met another Cuban woman who taught my mother to cook with Mexican ingredients. During those six months that we waited for our visas, my mother hustled for food during the day, returning to feed us in the late evenings. Meanwhile, my siblings and I fought constantly, driving my mother crazy.

I discovered Mexico had more than two television channels, and that the government didn't control what was shown, as they had in Cuba. The number of options mesmerized me and helped me cope with the changes I was experiencing. Eventually, the time came to leave Mexico, and this time, I was excited because I knew we were going to be with my father forever, or so I thought.

After arriving in Los Angeles and meeting my father's family in Torrance, we saw very little of him. My mother worked every day, so we were often on our own.

My next hurdle was learning the English language. I learned a hard and painful lesson that the languages were very different. When I went to take my first shower in America, I saw the "H" and "C" on the knobs. Thinking the "C" stood for caliente (hot), I turned the "H" faucet on, and the water came out scalding. I froze with confusion and stood there as boiling water poured over my head, arms, and legs. I ended up in the hospital for six weeks with third-degree burns. My long hair that covered most of my body prevented the burns from being worst. Every three days I would get scrubbed to help my cells regenerate. The pain was severe, and my insecurities deepened throughout my childhood and into my adulthood.

My Adult Life

As life went on, the tragedies continued. I suffered from excruciating migraines, and in 2002 I had severe joint pain, backaches, and more. I was diagnosed with endometriosis and severe anemia. I didn't have time to be ill. I was a single parent with three small children under the age of ten and one failed marriage. For 26 years, I was a caregiver to a brother with AIDS Dementia and a mother who was quadriplegic with numerous health issues.

I became a "human doer." I didn't have time to think about my pain; I was focused on everyone else's. I never thought about what I needed; I did everything for everyone else. For 47 years, I ignored all of my health and emotional issues.

My brother passed away, and my daughters eventually created their own lives and moved out one at a time. My mom passed after 27 years of care. Once they were gone, I did not know what to do with all of my time, effort, and energy. I believed that I had no identity; I was nobody's daughter, mother, sister, or wife. I became an empty nester.

I had been continually doing for others for most of my life; that was my purpose, my meaning. Now I had to find who I was. I had never felt so helpless, powerless, and hopeless.

Someone recommended that I see a psychiatrist, who explained that fibromyalgia was stress induced. The doctor suggested that my mom's death was the tipping point. Culturally, I was conditioned not to talk about my problems or express any emotions. I learned to suppress all my feelings of pain; but by not expressing myself, I accelerated my physical decline.

I saw another psychiatrist, but the prescribed medication kept me in a fog. I would forget words, get lost on my way home, and become depressed. That doctor suggested that I see a psychologist.

Throughout the years I tried many different therapies like biofeedback, acupuncture, physical therapy, floating therapy, and TENS units (a muscle stimulation device). I practiced mindfulness. I saw an herbalist and an audiologist. I tried all of those Eastern medicines after Western medicine had failed me. I ran out of options. I finally decided to surrender my healing to God.

During those 18 months, the psychologist focused on my childhood and the trauma I had experienced. This included my dad's alcoholism, my parent's toxic relationship, the abusive environment, and not being able to express our feelings with anyone, even amongst ourselves. Our experiences make us who we are, how we feel, think, and behave. I needed to heal and overcome what I had gone through to become whole.

I had spent the previous year reading books, talking to people, and doing anything I could to find an answer to my physical and emotional pain. My problem was that I didn't know where to look. I ended up thinking that I wasn't strong enough, that I couldn't let go of the toxic people in my life; that I needed them.

Then this wonderful man at the coffee shop came into my life, Michael Oden. I believed that I didn't deserve him, that he was too good to be true. My friend's energy and disposition had a very calming effect on me. I remember thinking at first that he must be a serial killer playing a part!

I built this emotional brick wall to protect myself from the trauma of leaving Cuba. As we got to know each other, he began to mentor and guide me on how to understand my pain, heal it, and to believe in myself. This would be my journey of self-discovery.

Michael taught me the 7-Step System to Self-Discovery, Awareness, and Empowerment, a methodology he developed. The steps can be used in any situation to give clarity and understanding of the moment. I felt hopeless because I had been diagnosed with fibromyalgia. Once you are labeled with a diagnosis, you either succumb to the illness, or you fight it. The emotional toll from my past had drained me of all my energy. I had to fight the disease, even though I didn't accept it.

I started to listen to this man that the universe placed in my life. At first, I struggled with the seven steps. What would my family and friends think of my new changes? The generational curses and culture shaming were so strong that I didn't think I was going to be able to break away from them. He continued to encourage me, and I am grateful and blessed that he has been there every step of the way. Now we are business partners, and I teach others what he taught me.

Here are three steps out of the seven that had the most impact on my life:

Step 1: Understanding. Comprehending the effect each event had and the meaning I was giving to each experience. I applied this step only after my mother's death. After she died, the generational curse was lifted. I no longer felt suffocated and began to believe in myself. I was emotionally free, and I stopped allowing other people's opinions to determine my choices.

Step 2: Acceptance. I need to be at peace with my past. Stop punishing myself for finding ways to survive. My choices were the best for me at the time. I began to accept responsibility for my behavior. I could only do what I knew in each moment.

Step 3: Value-shift. Changing my beliefs and behavior to be more life-affirming. If I wanted to be happy, I had to think positively about myself and ignore what other people thought about me. I needed to get rid of old beliefs. If my choices did not hurt other people, I did not have to worry. In the past, I would spend months feeling horrible. Now with the value-shift, I feel like a metal curtain has lifted.

I am grateful and blessed that Michael has been there for me every step of the way. He taught me about myself and the human condition, and about how to love myself and accept me for who I am, not what others want me to be. I am now joyful and empowered to teach what I have learned. Everything we do and say is about meeting our needs. What need is being met at the time that we exhibit specific behavior, either life-affirming or life-diminishing?

If I had never met him, I would not have been able to experience the wonderful things about myself that I have learned. He showed me how to be strong, how to believe that I could do whatever I decided to do. I now have awareness, understanding, and acceptance of my past, which empowers me to shift my beliefs and create a new outlook. I know the effect of being raised in an intense environment and now have the tools to be empowered to change.

Today is the beginning of the second chapter of my life. I am ready to show up the best way that I can. I'm ready to share what I've learned with others, to pay it forward.

If you are ready to find inner peace and joy, look for a tribe or another individual, like I did, who supports your journey and encourages you to evolve into the beautiful person you are meant to be.

Here are the three best self-discoveries I can give you:

- Deal with the impact of your childhood pain as soon as you become aware of it.
- Be willing to adjust, to acknowledge, and accept. Think of it as an adventure.
- It doesn't matter how long it takes you to shift your mindset as long as you do it!

Alina J. Ugas
The Truth Seeker

Alina Ugas

Alina, who was born in Santiago de Cuba, grew up as the third child in a very strict Cuban household. At the age of nine, her family migrated to Los Angeles, California, where they began to live the American dream.

With over 35 years' experience, Alina is a Licensed Practitioner of NLP, National Certified Recovery Coach, motivational speaker, workshop facilitator and trainer, and has a passion for helping others discover the "WHY" of their emotional decisions and self-destructive behaviors. After years of working with clients who battled drug addiction, anger issues, and eating disorders, Alina helped craft the development of The Needs Based Method®. This proven technique of getting to the individual's specific needs that have not been met has an 85% success rate. She believes that we all should "Think to be Different®."

Alina's commitment to the belief that coaching is not only a necessary life tool but a business tool as well led her, along with her partner, to start their own family business, Final Step International. Alina's vision is for all people to move forward with confidence, fully awake, and live consciously in the moment in order to live the life they desire.

You can contact Alina at www.TNBMTraining.com

CHAPTER 12

Be Fearless
by Luis Bolinao

I remember everything so clearly, like it was yesterday. All of my
life was in front of me. At 25 years old, I was a nurse who liked to
party with friends, be with my girlfriend, and travel. But that was
before we got the news about my younger sister, Anne Michelle.

Growing up, Michelle was my best friend. If I had an issue with
anything, she was the first person I told. Of course, we had our brother
and sister moments and fought. Even though Michelle was never the
type to back down from an argument, she was the nicest person you
could meet. Strong-willed and ready to speak her mind, she often told
me how it was, even when it wasn't what I wanted to hear. I loved my
sister like a brother should. Looking back on my life, there have been
many amazing individuals I've met, but no one came close to
impacting me like Michelle.

The moment I found out that she had stage-four brain cancer was
the day my life changed forever.

At the time, we both lived with our parents in Koreatown, a
neighborhood in Los Angeles. After a week of her staying with a
friend after work and not coming home, I called her.

She apologized and told me she had been suffering from a headache for days. That was unusual for her. She was not the type to complain, so I knew something was seriously wrong. I told her to meet me at the emergency room.

Michelle walked into the ER in a red hoodie, looking down as she waited, obviously in severe pain. I had never seen her in such distress.

After hours of waiting and the usual battery of tests, she was diagnosed with sinusitis, given antibiotics and painkillers, and sent home. I was so relieved. I took her home, thinking that everything was all right and she would soon be better.

After two days of bed rest, I thought she'd be better, but when I went to check on her, she looked so different. She was confused, her face was drooping, and her headache was back. At first I was in denial that what I was seeing was serious, but after speaking with her more, I knew she was not right. When I asked her if she wanted to go back to the ER, she said yes; that was unusual for her, so we rushed to the hospital.

Back at the ER, we waited anxiously. Although I was a nurse at the time, being there with my sister, I felt uneasy. Hours later we were called to see the doctor. He gave us his diagnosis: Michelle had a brain tumor, which explained her symptoms of confusion, facial drooping, and chronic headache. He continued, saying that she would need emergency surgery to remove the tumor.

Feeling as weak as I'd ever felt, I excused myself from the room and found a corner in which to cry. I blamed myself for not noticing her symptoms sooner and was confused about the previous diagnosis of sinusitis. I was scared. I felt lost, but I also knew that I had to be strong for my sister.

When the doctor saw me crying and stopped to check on me, I told him that my sister had become worse because of me. He guaranteed me that it was not my fault. After we talked, he sent my sister to prepare for the surgery. The tumor needed to be removed immediately.

Waiting for the surgery, however, took the better part of the day. By the time she was finally wheeled into the operating room, friends and family had gathered to wait with us. Those eight hours of her surgery were the longest of my life. I'd never felt so helpless. I went to the hospital chapel for most of the time, alternately crying and praying.

When the surgeon finally came to give us the news, he told us the tumor had been removed, and the surgery was successful. We were all so excited. Until…

He told us they would do tests on the tumor to find out if it is cancerous or not. After a week of waiting, we found out that she had a rare brain cancer called glioblastoma multiforme. The doctor told us that she had about two years to live, and prognosis on this type of cancer is very low. We were devastated, but we remained hopeful. We kept fighting.

After a few days of recovery, Michelle went home. We hoped that everything would go back to normal.

Over the next few months things went well, despite multiple doctor's appointments and chemo and radiation treatments. Her brain scars were healing, and she was tolerating her medicine well. She had started to go to the gym again and began to pick up part-time nursing shifts.

Then one day everything changed. While at the gym, Michelle had a seizure. After a 911 call, she was taken to the hospital where they did the usual tests. After waiting again for hours in the ER, we got the news that there was another tumor. Emergency surgery was again performed successfully. With a sense of déjà vu, we felt like we were back at square one, like we had taken two steps forward and ten steps back.

The emotional roller coaster was tough. We didn't know what to expect anymore. Michelle was prescribed stronger meds and more aggressive chemo. Some days we felt she was getting better; some days we didn't. What we did understand was that every moment with her was precious. So we went on multiple vacations and enjoyed our time together to the fullest.

As each day passed, Michelle became more physically and mentally challenged. She began to lose her hair, then her ability to walk, and then she became incontinent. Eventually, she needed a wheelchair. Finally, she was bedridden. I felt like I was losing my sister slowly every day. I was also losing hope each day, clinging to my faith.

Then, during one of her regular check-ups, the doctor confirmed that she had another tumor. This time the doctor advised our family that the tumor was inoperable and that we should put her in hospice care. The word "hospice" jumped out from the nursing notes.

Added to everything else, being a nurse during my sister's illness was one of the hardest parts of my life. I struggled to live life, thinking that I would lose my sister soon. Looking back, I still can't believe I survived the trauma of her loss. At the time, I really had no choice but to accept it. What else could I do?

Michelle had another major seizure but this time she was in severe pain, so they kept her at the hospital. Unable to recover from that, she soon passed away. I felt deep pain, and at the same time was relieved that she was no longer suffering. She had fought hard for 18 months.

Twelve days later, my son Luis Jr. was born. Life moves in mysterious ways, balancing unspeakable sorrow with unbelievable joy.

During the year and a half that Michelle was sick, I learned so much about life and death and who I was. For one, I gained a sense of urgency. Growing up, I was a happy-go-lucky guy. All I did was work and party on my days off. Although I was making good money nursing, I didn't really have a sense of purpose. After Michelle passed, I realized that I could be doing more than working to make money.

On her deathbed, Michelle said that all she wanted was to live. Unfortunately, she didn't have a choice, but I did.

I Learned How to Grieve

I wish I could tell you that I handled Michelle's death well, but I didn't. There were too many emotions going through me, both good and bad, and I didn't know how to deal with them. I chose to cover them up with partying and drinking.

I also had to make a big adjustment to fatherhood. I wanted to be the best dad ever, but my grief got in the way. My mindset that only crazy people got help with their mental problems kept me isolated, and I buried it with alcohol and violent behavior. Four months later, I knew something had to change. My mother-in-law introduced me to network marketing, and I knew that this was the vehicle to make a change in my life.

I decided to become the best version of myself and undertook personal development daily. Following inspirational people such as Les Brown, Jim Rohn, and Tony Robbins, I attended personal development seminars. I surrounded myself with winners.

One of them heard about my sister's passing and recommended that I take a grief recovery class. It was the beginning of a time of healing for me. My wife and I also decided to go to counselling so that we could be healthy together. I am so thankful to my recovery coach, Mikki, for teaching me how to grieve properly. It changed my life. I could finally move forward and live my true dream of being an entrepreneur.

There were other valuable lessons I learned during this process. My perception of time changed. I learned that tomorrow isn't really a promise, and I spent even more time with my family.

I was reminded that health is precious. When Michelle got sick, a lot of things were no longer critical, except for her health. Everything seemed to stop. My job didn't matter, money didn't matter, what car I drove didn't matter, and material possessions didn't matter. The only thing that was important was that she lived.

Realizing how essential health really is, I began to prioritize it. I exercised up to five days a week. I decided to eat better, use natural products, and became more aware of what I consumed and wore. I pursued a health and wellness business, and I now thrive on educating people about the importance of physical and mental health.

Michelle's death also amplified how important family is in life. When I was younger, I thought most people lived to be 90 years old and traumatic deaths only happened in the movies. Losing my sister at the age of 24 changed my perspective.

Realizing that anyone can be taken at any time, I cherish every single moment with those I love. I decided to leave nursing and pursue a home-based business so that I could have more control over my time. Nursing was a great career, but I was working long hours away from family and friends.

Probably the biggest thing I've changed in my life is that I am fearless with my decisions. I take calculated risks now. I get on stage to speak, having overcome my once-crippling fear of being in front of audiences. I make investments. I do video marketing for my online presence. I've fought through my fear of being judged. I really believe that I reached the top one percent of my network marketing company with no previous business, selling, or marketing experience by being fearless.

I've created a bigger life for myself by facing my fears and taking action. Grief has propelled me to the top. I am now bold and don't care what people might think of me.

I feel like I was given a second chance. I've been able to unlearn the habits and beliefs that limited me in the past. I've expanded my perspective by being around people who lift me up and whose successes I want to emulate. Staying away from negative people in my environment has helped me level up in life. Michelle's life – and death – taught me to live fully in every moment, and that is what I've chosen to do.

Instead of letting fear paralyze you, feel the fear and do it anyway. If you want to pursue a different career, go for it. If you want to start a business, start it. If you want to become a motivational speaker, put in the work and just do it. Don't let other people's opinions hold you back. Life becomes so much more worth living when you live it fully.

I want to leave you with three key things that changed my life:

- Be okay with the grieving process. It is good to cry, to be sad, and sometimes down. I believe that if we can be happy, we can also be sad as well.
- Don't miss out on the second chances in life. Opportunities will come, and you can't be afraid to take the risk.
- Love those closest to you. Make an effort to be a part of their lives.

I know that Michelle is looking down and smiling. I wrote this chapter to honor her and what she taught me through her life and death. Now it is time for you to take action.

Growth happens when you face your fears. Be fearless.

Luis Bolinao

Luis Bolinao

Luis Bolinao is a father, husband, and committed entrepreneur. Growing up in the Philippines as the eldest of four, he learned to take on big responsibilities at a young age.

In 2005, his parents and siblings decided to move to California; he was 15 years old. The transition was hard since he was ready to graduate and go to college in the Philippines. In the U.S., Luis had to go back to the 10th grade and start over. He endured the setback and graduated from high school and then went on to become a nurse.

In his second year of nursing, he met his future wife and they share a stepdaughter and a son. During this time, his dear younger sister Michelle passed away at 24 years of age.

After months of therapy and grieving, he began to use her death as a motivation to want to do more. He was introduced to network marketing where he could work less but have more time and freedom.

After that, he decided to take the road of entrepreneurship. Five years later, Luis and his wife still continue to grow multiple businesses. He strives to be someone his kids, his family, and his sister Michelle can be proud of.

Instagram: luisbolinao
labolinao@gmail.com

CHAPTER 13

Grow Beyond Your Shadows
by Stacey Randolph

*W*hen I was asked recently to reflect on overcoming the biggest obstacle in my life, one thing stood out in my memory. It was 18 years ago when I stepped out on faith to trust God's plan in my life. Despite being a 26-year-old single parent of two small daughters, I decided to pursue my dream and relocate 800 miles from New Jersey to Georgia.

During this time, my girlfriends invited me to go to Atlanta with them for the weekend. I decided to accept the invitation to take a girls' trip to Atlanta, Georgia, because I wanted to experience new territory and venture out beyond my surroundings. My intentions were two-fold – I definitely believed in having a good time in addition to taking care of business.

While all my friends were still asleep from partying all night, I went to a job fair to see what employment opportunities were available in the area. I was immediately offered a job with Bell South on the spot. The only setback was my pay would be cut in half for the same position I already held at Verizon in New Jersey.

I had not planned on moving at the time, but as I gave the offer more thought, I realized this move might be the change I needed. At the time, I was emotionally empty and financially strapped after the loss of my daughter's father in a motorcycle accident in 1999 and my then current boyfriend's murder in 2001. Most importantly, I needed this alone time to do some soul-searching to try and figure out who I was.

It only took a moment to realize that what I needed was a fresh start, so I returned home to New Jersey, resigned from my position at Verizon with two weeks' notice and started to pack up my belongings to move.

I knew no one in Georgia, no family, friends or contacts, but something in my spirit led me to believe this move would hold the key to God's promise of happiness in my life. My relatives and friends thought I was losing my mind and were animatedly against my decision to move. Despite their concerns, comments, threats, tears, and pleas, I was convinced Georgia held the key to my success. Something within my spirit believed that the move would place me one step closer to owning my dream life.

Fourteen days later, I had a full U-Haul but no cell phone, no savings, and only a virtual tour of my new apartment. Despite the negative obstacles and life setbacks, I was determined to move and turn my mess into success, so I hit the Jersey turnpike and never looked back.

Many people thought relocating to Georgia was me running away from my issues, and I would have to agree. However, the move was an opportunity to escape the dark shadows of insecurity and inadequacy that had been following me for years.

These shadows would have me believe I was a worthless single mother with two children and a GED. I would often devalue myself, falling prey to toxic and abusive relationships. Some of these left me with visible wounds that would heal, while other injuries would go unseen, lingering in my spirit for years.

The shadow of fear has been my biggest enemy in life. It left me with fear of failure, abandonment, being loved, change, and even success. The crazy thing about me running and relocating to Georgia to escape my shadows is the closer I got to the state, the bigger my shadows became.

In science class, they taught us that the closer you are to the light, the more substantial your shadow becomes. I never realized that basic concept would apply to my real-life experiences.

After moving to Georgia, I still faced adversity. Upon arriving to my new home, I was astonished to find out that it did not match up to the images I saw online. The apartment was in the rear of an unrenovated section, with no exterior lighting at night. In addition, the apartment was infested with several guests (bugs) that were not listed on my lease as occupants. In light of the uninvited occupants, I chose not to unpack my furnishings and quickly searched for a new place.

Regardless of the setback, I pushed through my fear of change, staying committed to my decision to stay in Georgia, and after a two week search I found a new complex with a rent-controlled, three-bedroom apartment in a gated community with loads of amenities.

I began to warm up to the idea of living in the South and became excited about turning into a 'Jersey Peach.' Within two months of my move date, I was set to bring my little princesses − my daughters − down to join me.

Over the next few years, I went through a period of hibernation and healing with my babies. I connected with a local church and built new relationships. I did the deep work required of me and fell in love with myself. I began to read Iyana Vanzant's daily inspirations, exercised (and everyone knows how I hate it), joined the dance ministry in my church, and even became celibate.

I worked on improving my credit and faced my fear of other people's opinions of me and my fear of failure. I took the time to work on freeing myself from the judgment and shadows of my past. For the first time in my life, I planted strong spiritual roots that allowed me to forgive people, places, and things that had hurt me. Most importantly, I forgave myself for some of the bad choices I made in life.

This time of transformation was much needed. I remember riding past local subdivisions with my daughters and going inside the model homes with dreams of purchasing one in the future. Each of us would pick out our favorite room, discussing how we would decorate it and live happily ever after.

I would often write down my desires in life and place them in my Bible under Psalms 121:1-2, "I will lift my eyes to the hills from whence cometh my help, my help cometh from the Lord." I wanted a good-paying job, a great husband, a lovely house, a son, a dog, to be skinny, a good retirement account, a nice car, and an annual vacation. In short, I wanted to live the good life.

During this time of growth, healing, and evolution, I became allergic to corporate America. That's right, allergic, in the literal sense, in that I would become sick and had severe migraines every time I arrived at work. My physical reaction to my hostile, unhappy work environment became so severe that I was terminated from my telecommunication sales position while on disability.

The financial setback cost me my beautiful 3-bedroom apartment, and I ended up sleeping on an air mattress in my babysitter's living room for three weeks with my daughters until I could find another job.

Despite this setback, I was not about to go back to New Jersey empty-handed and humbled. I decided then that if I moved back to

New Jersey, it would be on the high side of life and not as a failure. It would be by choice and not forced upon me.

For the next two years, I humbled myself and took a few low paying jobs in the insurance industry, putting myself on a peanut butter and jelly diet. I found another rent-controlled apartment and took in a renter to make ends meet. I'd often have to pick up my daughters at lunch and bring them back to work because I couldn't afford full-day childcare.

Humility is a step in life that is vital to your success, and I have learned the hard way that if I cannot humble myself, the universe will! I had to face my shadow of pride as I have learned, "Pride comes before a fall." (Proverbs 16:8) I now understand that sometimes you have to take a few steps backward and complete your missing assignments before you can leap forward. Fortunately, leaping forward is what came next.

The universe finally rewarded me for a job well done, and in 2004 I was given the opportunity to open my first insurance agency. The only obstacle was that I needed $50,000, and my checking account statement said I was $49,950 shy of the required amount to open it. Still, I went through the interview process, pretending I had all the money and that I was vetting the insurance company.

I prayed day and night, asking everyone I knew to invest in me. I worked on my credit again and increased my score 230 points after bankruptcy. I even led my prospective employer to believe that they were only one of my options, and I would get back to them with my decision. I kept my faith and became my number one brand ambassador, believing in the power of me.

Pressing through my naysayers and removing myself from the peanut gallery of Debbie-downers around me, the answer then came to me. All I needed to do was buy a great piece of real estate and use some of the equity to open my agency. Sometimes you need to show that you are no longer hungry for help, that you have evolved to the next level. You are the hungry hunter who can show them better than you can tell them.

My ideas finally lined up with divine timing as the real-estate market was booming, and there were creative loan products available to second-chance contenders like myself. I purchased my first home after bankruptcy for $125,000, with almost $85,000 in equity. Four months after closing, I went back and refinanced my house, and then immediately contacted my insurance agency recruiter and told him I decided to accept their offer and open my agency.

I started training in January, 2005, and opened my first agency on March 1, 2005. I went on to obtain my real estate license in 2008 and purchased my second agency in 2015. I have surpassed my 2002 desires and am now a business owner with five loving children, a beautiful home, nice vehicles, and I travel once a month.

I offer mentorship programs for aspiring entrepreneurs and working moms, do motivational speaking and business consulting, am still sexy, was married for over 12 years, and I am currently 45 and fabulous. The list I wrote down in my Bible manifested in my life once I faced my shadows.

Today, I am a firm believer in the power of prayer, belief, and karmic justice. Regardless of how big your Goliath may be, keep praying, believing, and doing right by others, and God will turn things around for you!

I am happy that I stepped out on faith and grew beyond my shadows. If you are caught in the shadow stages of life, face your fear of failure and align your energy with a spiritual connection. Have faith and believe in a higher power working behind the scenes on your behalf to manifest the desires of your heart. Once there, you will be truly free to progress forward in life without regrets, living a full and abundant life filled with happiness and joy in your heart.

You must also have endurance and courage to face the storms you will encounter; the same type of patience it takes to race to the top of the highest mountain. It's never about the start but about the finish. When you are walking uphill against the obstacles of life, you must align your heart and mind to be lifted up beyond your obstructions.

If your mind and heart are committed to being elevated, then your outcome will also be raised. If you keep your eye on the prize and honestly believe you are a winner, then you will be. I often say that I can only run if I'm being chased because that is when my adrenaline and fear kicks in. Utilizing that same adrenaline and fear toward beating the odds in life and obtaining your goals is exactly what will push you to the finish line.

As a life-long salesperson, I have learned that the best salespeople are masters at managing objections. They have learned that objections don't matter. Applying this basic sales concept to all your objections can yield amazing victories in life.

Sometimes in life, you must be willing to let go of familiar ground and discover unfamiliar territory. Planting your feet in fertile ground does not mean your dreams will not need to be nurtured and fertilized. Nor does it mean that you won't need to aerate the soil and make sure you are planting your ideas in a safe and prosperous place.

The first soil you have to purge is what is planted in your head. Once you do that, everything in life will begin to blend. You are in control of your destiny and the canvas you paint. If you don't like the painting you started, move to a new canvas with new colors and images. When you paint this mosaic, remember to minimize the shadows that block your light.

Owning your dream is not always easy. We live in a world of the constant duality of good and bad, and you must be aware of the unique balance required for your seeds to grow. You must learn about yourself, your environment, and your triggers to maintain that healthy balance. Despite all the roadblocks and moments of stagnation, always find your inner strength to push forward. Not toward the person you see right now in the mirror, but the person you have the potential to be. Trust that trouble won't last, and the law of attraction will work with you to manifest greatness.

Grow in your moment and take breaks to self-reflect, strategize, heal, and grow. Doing so creates strong roots that will not be moved by the winds of life. The darker the moments you face, the deeper the roots grow to withstand the next storm.

Never doubt yourself and your ability to turn your mess into a success! Let go of the negative events in your life, as your branches should never be larger than your trunk. Only hold on to the lessons you've learned as badges you have earned.

Remember, you are designed to soar high like an eagle, never looking back or worrying about the snakes you meet because they are not designed to survive in the same elevations you occupy. Lift your head high and let go of your baggage and your burdens. Eagles fly forward, and as they rise above the clouds, they can look down and be reminded of the shadows they have overcome.

Life is too short to live in regret, so seize opportunities as if they are your last. Keep an open mind and open heart to allow blessings to come in.

I cannot say that I'm completely free from the shadows in my life, but I continue to soar to new heights, with newfound skills to grow beyond the shadows that chase me. Now I treat those shadows like a game of hide and seek. They hide, but I find them quickly and "tag" them out of my life, and you can too!

Stacey Randolph

Stacey Randolph

Stacey Randolph is an ambitious, high performing sales professional with a strong 20-year background in Insurance, Sales Management, New Business Development, and Real Estate. A Serial Entrepreneur with vast experience regarding business ownership from acquisitions to mergers, Stacey is the owner of multiple Allstate insurance agencies in the metro Atlanta area. As a proud second-generation insurance agent, she has received numerous awards by the insurance industry and notably is licensed in multiple states.

This proud mother of five and published author knows what it takes to run a successful business and build a legacy for her family. Stacey is an activist in her own right and is always an avid supporter in the walk against gun violence, childhood illness, mental health awareness, domestic violence, and financial literacy to name a few.

Stacey loves community involvement, and serves on the board of directors as well as is an active member of Safe Table Talks, PADV, Heaven Sent Hearts Foundation, Red Bottoms in Business Movement, and the Allstate Purple Purse Campaign, all of which are leading organizations and non-profits within her community.

www.staceyrandolph-castillo.com

CHAPTER 14

Write Your Dream Check
by Paul White

*M*y life has been filled with unexpected twists and turns; yet through it all I have somehow found a way to continue to learn, grow, and pass it on. Many people have inspired me to work daily at becoming my best self. However, my greatest inspiration has always been my dear, sweet grandmother.

Mrs. Mary Lewis was a powerful woman of high standards, great respect, and brilliant creativity. She knew how to provide those around her with a homecourt advantage. Even though she didn't have many material possessions, she was rich beyond measure. When you were in her presence, you felt an abundance of encouragement, wisdom, and most of all, love.

I can vividly remember observing my grandmother closely while spending quality time with her around the house. I gained some of the greatest life lessons that at the time seemed very simple, however, when I look back, extraordinary occurrences unfolded right before my very eyes.

For example, she would direct my cousin and me to go into the kitchen to see what was left for her to be able to prepare for a meal. With authority and an all-knowing confidence she would say, "You children go in the kitchen and tell me what you can find, and then I'll tell you what special meal I am going to make for you!"

In great anticipation, expectancy, and excitement we would begin exploring the cabinets, the countertops, and the refrigerator for the raw ingredients that we knew she could and would combine for a magical culinary experience that we would soon share as a family. On most days we might find a few slices of bread, a couple of eggs, some beans, and a few other minimal, bare necessities. No matter what we found, Grandma Mary would somehow always create something extraordinary that would fill our bellies and warm our hearts.

I was amazed that she always had a 'glass half full' mentality and the ability to have a positive outlook amid challenging times. She mastered the art of making much out of the minuscule. That mindset has helped me tremendously throughout my adult life. Oftentimes, we get overwhelmed with life, thinking that we are limited because we may not have several degrees, thousands of connections, or millions of dollars. I have learned that we only need "just enough"– just enough to allow us to implement and employ the lessons learned and listen closely to those who are willing to give us the tools for winning. The possibilities are unlimited when we are willing to "do what we can, with what you have, from where you are" just as Theodore Roosevelt said in his famous quote:

> *"You may just have a little bit of faith, with a couple of dashes of hope and several cups of perseverance mixed with a powerful idea or desire…and that just might be more than enough to make your dreams come true."*

Hold On to Your Dream

I have had a fascination with automobiles ever since I was a small child. My passionate desire was to learn everything about the different types of makes and models. Studying the various designs and hearing the roar of an engine was one of the most exhilarating experiences for me. As a result, I have always known that I wanted to work in the automotive industry in some capacity as a career choice.

Interestingly, since I was very athletic and was extremely good at most sports, it would often be suggested that I pursue professional athletics. The prospect of fame and fortune being bestowed on me due to my natural abilities was intriguing and caused me to work hard to create that reality. I knew I wanted to do something great in the world, I just was unsure of which path would ultimately be the best for me to take.

Sometimes one opportunity may fall apart, causing us to be rerouted back to our initial desires due to that mandatory detour which ultimately works out to be our divine destiny. Always remember that the appearance of failure does not have to be final. When my professional sports career did not unfold in the way I thought it would, I still had my original dream buried in my heart, waiting to be revived again.

My love for the automotive industry was instilled at a very young age and my father played a big role in that. He was the original "car lover" and it was passed down to me from him. I set a big goal to own a car dealership one day and then I began the rigorous journey to making it become a reality.

The $5 Million Dollar Check

I quickly became very successful as a young adult in sales, and then moved up into management. Displaying exceptional work ethic, discipline, people skills and leadership was almost second nature to me. I had found myself in the zone of doing what I loved on a day-today basis and doing it extremely well. I soon became an ownership partner of a dealership and they paid me handsomely, to say the least.

In the midst of this massive success ride that I was on, I felt as if I could conquer the world and that anything I touched would turn to gold. As the old folks would say, "I was a bit too big for my own britches!"

After much soul searching and contemplation, I decided I would take a huge leap of faith and go out on my own by acquiring my own store of which I would be the majority owner. This made so much sense to me at the time, considering how well everything was working in my favor, so I went for it with everything that I had.

I was able to create incredible momentum and check off some significant accomplishments at a very early age. That turned out to be a tremendous source of blessings for me. The grandiose actions I engaged in allowed me to go through some mountain top success peaks and some low valleys of learning along the way. Yet each time, good or bad, I was fortunate enough to be able to regroup so that I could rebuild and continue to make it happen.

Inspiration can come to you from the seemingly most inconceivable of places. One day while sitting in my office, I decided that I was going to utilize a bit of my Grandma Mary's manifesting power. In what would prove to be an act of Courage, Confidence, and Commitment, I wrote a check to myself for five million dollars. As I was writing it out, I knew in every fiber of my being that I would be able to cash it one day. It was the year 2000 when I initially facilitated this act of faith. I carried it around with me every day as a reminder of the vision that I had to make a reality. The takeaway from that exercise in faith and focus is you can accomplish whatever you keep at the front of your mind. That check haunted me and helped me to become the person capable of cashing it.

The only person that will truly pay you what you are worth will most likely be you. When I came to that realization, I was then willing to get into the driver's seat of my success to make the things that I desired and dreamed of to happen for myself. Even before I had a complete understanding of the requirements that came with taking on that responsibility, I committed myself to figure it out; all the while I was in motion to bring it about.

Writing yourself a check and then finding a way to cash it is a simple yet powerful exercise. It sets a clear intention and declares a specific amount of effort and execution you are willing to exert towards financial progression you are in the process of building for you and your dreams.

Make sure that the amount of the check that you write for yourself is an amount that resonates with you and what you want. The check amount does not have to be for five million dollars. Choose an amount that is going to stretch you and inspire you to work hard to achieve it. However, not an amount that is so very high that you will subconsciously consider it to be impossible.

I knew that millions would be a huge stretch for me to achieve, but at the same time I knew within my heart that the Great Les Brown was right when he said, "Your dream is possible!" The power of Possibility is one of the greatest gifts we can utilize. Possibility stretches you and causes you to get out of the comfort zone of mediocrity and strive to reach areas that before you considered out of reach. As long as it's possible, it can be accomplished. That's the mindset I approached cashing that check and all the big wins of my life with.

It was with great joy, gratitude, and enthusiasm that I was able to cash that check six years later in 2006. It was one of the proudest moments in my life. I will never forget how it made me feel to finally accomplish my dream of that magnitude. I felt invincible and it was as if I was on top of the world. Little did I know just how quickly the tides of life could shift, and within two years I would, unfortunately, lose it all.

My Entire World Flipped Upside-Down

I watched in disbelief as the whole world changed during the unexpected recession, and it not only affected me financially but emotionally, mentally, spiritually, and physically as well. It was the first time that I can admit that I was professionally knocked out and I fell flat on my face, with very little hope of being resuscitated. Mike Tyson once said, "Everyone has a plan until they get hit in the mouth."

The economy took a dramatic turn for the worst. All of the successful techniques that I had relied on in the past were no longer working in the new day that had fallen upon us. The economic catastrophe that ensued was so debilitating that it wiped out entire industries and devasted many businesses.

My business rapidly plummeted until it hit rock bottom. Out of options, I sold my remaining stock back to the guy that I was partnered with. At this point it had very little value and we still owed the bank. Getting out alive was my new game plan. It was a humiliating lesson to learn, but one I learned with equal parts humility and honesty.

I was in a time in my life where I began to question every decision that I had ever made, but particularly I continuously replayed over and over in my mind the day that I walked away from a business that paid me extremely well. Difficulty will make you second guess yourself and wonder if you were being faithful or vain when you made the decisions that brought you your demise.

During that depressively disappointing time, I felt as if I was surrounded by a cloud of failure. Even though I had accomplished my dreams and the loss I was facing was caused by external forces, I still felt like a failure. My grandmother's words rang true in my mind, "You are not a failure because you fail, you become a failure when you give up and stop trying." I had to take a tough inventory of my life. Then I had to decide which avenue to take to re-establish myself and also seriously contemplate if I would ever be able to bounce back again. But I knew failure was a non-option.

I had to refer back to life lessons from my grandmother, my father, Bishop T. D. Jakes, and Les Brown. When we find ourselves in the eye of the storms of life, it helps to tap into the power, inspiration, and wisdom of those that can uplift you when you need it the most. Give yourself what you need to grow through the toughest times of your life.

You must be willing to fight for yourself and your dream because no one is willing or obligated to fight on your behalf. You must be relentless and be comfortable with being uncomfortable. If plan A and plan B don't work out, then it's time to create your plan C, plan D, and even a plan E, if necessary.

For me, giving up was not an option because I could not let my grandma down. She had a tough life and never gave up because she had such a strong mindset. Grandma Mary could've thrown in the towel many times but never did. She always found a way even when there appeared to be no way to be found. She inspired me to always look for a way when there didn't seem to be one. "That's what winners do - they find a way or make a way."

Her wisdom was like an ever-flowing fountain that is still enriching my life, even today. She shared with me countless gems of knowledge, however, two particular instructions shaped my reality in a very profound way and still resonate with me today.

First, she told me to write my own story and second, to be adaptable while making the story become true. At that chaotic juncture of my life, I chose to sit down and ask myself some tough questions, "Who is Paul White, and what does he stand for?" I concluded that I didn't want to be that guy who walks into and out of a room without anyone ever noticing that I was there. I decided that I wanted to be a man of impact, influence, and integrity.

I observed that many people show up on Earth, stroll in and stumble out of life, yet never make it any better or touch anyone in a significant manner. I decided within myself that my life story would be greater than an average existence and I made a commitment to live a life of purpose, on purpose, for a purpose.

The thing that gives me goosebumps and motivates me more than anything else is making a difference in someone's life that may be on the precipice of giving up. I relish in taking that average person and showing them how to become good, then bringing that good person to greatness. I consider it being an agent of change in someone's life that not only impacts them, but their family as well. It only takes that one changed person in the family tree to create a whole new reality for the rest of the family members.

Being adaptable while writing my story was such a priceless and timeless experience. Businesses close oftentimes because they cannot adapt to the current changes and shifts of that industry. Therefore, I set a clear intention to stay relevant to the challenges and demands of the marketplace. I learned from the debacle of the last economic downturn how to be prepared and postured to weather the storms that we all may face in the process of living

New Beginnings

I needed to get back on my financial feet, so I moved to the East Coast and accepted the role as COO of a new group of great partners. In the meantime, I utilized that time to live below my means and continued to sharpen my skills professionally. This was not an easy thing to do because I had fallen so far into the pits of a sunken place. Yet the skills and knowledge I had acquired allowed me to still be able to offer enough value to the marketplace that I could get back on my feet.

I surmised if my grandma could move around on an uncarpeted floor that gave you splinters with just about every step to provide for her loved ones without complaining, then surely I could make do with what I had. I went on to accept another role where I was living conservatively and it opened an array of opportunities for me to show the automotive industry decision-makers what I was capable of doing. It was a great brand-building position for me.

I just kept moving on up until I became the president of AutoNation in Texas. That particular role allowed me to have a seat at the big table with key dealership leaders. It also positioned me to develop my voice and speak on stage about industry-specific issues and developments.

The four and a half years that I held that position as president had a huge influence on me in regard to finding a way to get back to my place of power. I'm working every day to getting closer to creating the greatest reality possible with the abundance of gifts and talents that I have been blessed to possess.

One dream that I was able to achieve in order help empower others was the formation of The Crest Community Care Program and the Sterling Community Care Program, where I donate cars to faith-based organizations and churches.

While residing in Texas, I was involved with a huge congregation and I donated ten cars to single-parent mothers who were committed to serving and supporting the church faithfully. Many of them had not had their own means of transportation, yet somehow found a way to participate and make a difference in the lives of others. The church chose who these recipients would be, and I would also donate money to the church every time a car was bought to fund this community empowerment project.

The other program I am proud of is designed to mentor children that come from challenged areas and tough upbringings. Even when I was but a child myself, I distinctly remember my grandma telling me that she was deeply concerned for the young people in her neighborhood. She knew that many of them had big dreams but lived in the wrong area that could make it very difficult for their dreams to grow. She wished they could see with their mind's eye past their circumstances and work hard to rise above all of the many obstacles in their way.

One of the main reasons why I work as diligently as I do is to make my Grandma Mary super proud of me so that she can smile down from heaven. I know that she would want me to give to those in need and work to empower the next generation – showing them that there is a better path and that they can live their dreams. I want to encourage you to be relentless with your goals and dreams. It may not happen when or how you think it should, but don't you ever give up. Find within yourself the courage to keep moving forward, and one day you will see the desires of your heart in full manifestation.

Do your dreams a favor and accept this challenge. Write a check out to yourself for an amount that would take your life to the next level. Maybe it won't be a dollar amount that you write, but perhaps you can write your dream on that check with specific details of what you want your life to be like. Then place the check in the front of your wallet or purse where you will be able to see it each time you open it. Carry your dream check with you until you can cash it in and then keep it in your purse/wallet as a reminder to always be grateful for the incredible blessings that you have been blessed to behold.

I am so very thankful for the love and guidance that was imparted within me as a child and I'm still understanding, applying, and demonstrating as an adult man.

Right now, as you have read these words from my story and my heart...another dream of mine has come true. That dream is to share with you the priceless gems of life that Grandma Mary left within me. Now do your part to actualize her loving wisdom within your own life and then pass it on!

Paul White

Paul White

Paul White is an award-winning speaker, author, and respected automotive executive. Since he was a kid working on his dad's car lots, he has had a deep desire to do and be his best. Over the past 20 years, he has led some of the nation's foremost organizations to new, record-setting heights.

Paul's hands-on work in every department of a dealership, his guidance of multi-store and multi-state operations, and his innovative approach to team building combine to give him invaluable perspective and skill that extend far beyond his industry.

Today, Paul serves as President and CEO of Sterling Motor Cars and is a sought-after speaker. He lives in the Washington D.C. Metro area.

pwhite@paulwhiteent.com
www.paulwhiteent.com
LinkedIn ~ paul-white-autoexec

CHAPTER 15

Turn Pain into Purpose
by Hillary Foster, MFT

*L*ike most young girls, I grew up with the notion that one day I would marry Prince Charming and live happily ever after. This was the dream I carried in my heart based on what society told me would make me happy. However, by the time I reached my early thirties, I had not found him, and in the eyes of many, there was something wrong with me.

Even though I desperately wanted to be married (as if that would magically solve all my problems), I wasn't surprised that I was still single in my thirties. I came from a divorced family, and on an unconscious level, getting married scared the crap out of me. Studies show that coming from a divorced family can result in a reluctance to commit, and that was me.

My parents split when I was 11 years old. I was confused, sad, and angry. I was very close to my father, and one day he was just gone with no explanation.

I later found out he was bipolar, but to my young, vulnerable heart, he had abandoned me when I needed him the most. My older sister also left for college, leaving a bigger hole in my heart. I compensated by retreating into my own little world.

I started to come out of my shell when I went to college and studied psychology. I wanted to know more about human behavior and why we do the things we do, but more importantly, I wanted to make sense of what happened in my own family.

I loved the learning but was challenged to apply it in my own life as I picked the wrong guy over and over again. Each time my heart was broken it reinforced my abandonment issues.

After getting my bachelor's degree in psychology, I went on to obtain my master's in clinical psychology and eventually was licensed as a marriage and family therapist. By my credentials, I was an expert in relationships.

Not long after settling into my private practice as a newly licensed therapist, it happened: I met Prince Charming. He was tall, dark, and handsome – every bit the part of my childhood fantasy.

I remember the moment we locked eyes as if it happened yesterday. I was standing in line for the restroom at a restaurant (so romantic), and our eyes met. My heart felt like it exploded in my chest. I remained calm on the inside but felt the blood rushing through my legs.

When it was my turn to go into the restroom, I made a deal with myself. If he were still there when I came out, I would walk by his table and say hello. I was so nervous, but at the same time, I felt compelled to do it – I was drawn to him.

Sure enough, when I came out, he was sitting there by himself. I quickly surveyed the area, making sure he wasn't with someone. Nope, there was only one glass at the table. I started toward him, and our eyes met again. He stood up and greeted me with a huge smile. Phew, what a relief! He asked me if I wanted to sit down and have a drink. I said, "Yes."

He was charming and charismatic, with just a dash of humility thrown in. The chemistry was palpable. The conversation flowed with ease, and I didn't want it to end. I never went back to the table where my friends were waiting for me.

They came to check on me several times, and I kept saying, "I'll be right over," but I never made it back. Time seemed to stand still until my friend called and asked, "Do you want a ride home?" I was confused, but then I looked up and saw that the restaurant was closed!

"Oh, my goodness. I have to go," I said to Prince Charming while we exchanged numbers.

He said he had "never met anyone like me." I was smitten. He told me he was going away for the weekend, and he would have asked me to go if he knew me better. I responded, "I would have said yes if I knew you better." We left it at that.

The next day, I met a friend for a spa day and told her about Prince Charming. She was skeptical, but then again, she always was. I didn't pay attention to her hesitancy.

When he returned from his weekend away, we had our first date at a delicious Thai restaurant. The food was amazing, but I could hardly eat due to my nervous energy. You know that feeling you get when your dreams are unfolding before your eyes? Yeah, that's what it felt like.

I couldn't wait to see him again, and he felt the same. From that day forward, we saw each other regularly.

Things progressed quickly. I was about to turn 34, and he was almost 12 years my senior, so it didn't seem unrealistic to be making plans for the future early in our relationship. After all, I had just met my soul mate! We saw each other nearly every day for the next year. We worked out together, enjoyed the same foods, traveled, and wanted similar things in life. The relationship seemed perfect. I knew in my heart this was the man for me.

A year into our relationship, he whisked me off to San Francisco and proposed. I was giddy with excitement. I couldn't believe the fairy tale was coming true. As we were preparing for our future together, I came across some paperwork that seemed strange. It stated that the woman he said was his aunt was really his biological mother. I was perplexed. Why would he lie to me about who his biological mother was?

I confronted him, and his explanation seemed plausible. His biological mother was schizophrenic, and I could relate because my father was bipolar. So I dismissed it, even though I had a sinking feeling in my gut. If he could lie about this, what other lies might he tell?

I didn't feel I could tell anyone about it. What would they think of me? This was my dream come true and I wouldn't do anything to ruin it, so I buried the feelings deep inside and resumed planning my dream life. My fiancé was very doting, taking me to fabulous dinners, on lavish trips, and buying me lovely gifts. We lived in Laguna Beach, California two blocks from the beach. What more could a girl ask for? We planned a very beautiful wedding and life together that was everything a girl had dreamed about.

Soon after we were married, we had the good fortune of becoming pregnant. I was so ecstatic and couldn't wait to be a mom. I was still settling into my role as a new wife and soon-to-be mother. Even though I was a marriage and family therapist, I didn't know much about how to have a successful relationship (my apologies to any clients I had in my early years). I knew the theories I had learned in school, but had zero practical application.

However, I was living in a state of bliss, knowing that we would work out any problems that came our way. I allowed my husband to take the lead on many things and assumed the role of a subservient wife, even though that was far from my nature of being an independent and typically outspoken woman.

A year into our marriage, we had a healthy, beautiful baby boy! As all you moms out there can relate, it is an exciting yet exhausting time. Like most new parents, we were clueless. The sleepless nights and draining days led to a disconnection between us. I chalked it up to a phase of being new parents and that we would soon get back on track. On top of being new parents and newlyweds, my mother-in-law needed full-time care due to complications from a stroke. Our plates were full!

I started to notice that my husband would leave early in the morning and come home late after our son was asleep. He was a real estate agent, and he would tell me he had clients or was working on a listing. I was knee-deep in childcare, so I didn't question it. He was my husband, and I trusted him.

Almost a year and a half later, we got pregnant with our second child. It was during this time that our first son was diagnosed with cerebral palsy. I couldn't wrap my head around it because I had a normal vaginal delivery with no complications. I was devastated and also very pregnant, so I did what any other mom would do in the same situation: I got to work and made a plan for his healing.

With lots of physical therapy, our son made great progress and finally started walking by the age of two. However, we weren't out of the woods, yet. When he entered preschool, he was also diagnosed with Autism. I felt defeated once again, but I knew that I had to do what was necessary to get him the best treatment possible.

After our second son was born, I was completely overwhelmed with all the duties of caring for a newborn and the challenges our other son faced, and I was barely surviving. I tried to hold onto the thought that things would get better. My husband and I were two ships in the night. I went to bed early as I was breastfeeding; he would stay up late and leave early in the morning. I tried to be a good wife and balance all the things that were going on. I naively assumed that we would reconnect once things settled down a bit.

That all changed one day when I found a note with a reservation for a hotel in Los Angeles when he told me he was taking a trip with the guys to Las Vegas.

My heart sank down to my stomach and that same feeling of knowing came back to me.

I chose not to confront my husband as I knew he would lie about it. I kept obsessively checking the reservation as if magically I could get my old life back. I knew that wasn't a possibility, so I hired a private investigator.

Later that evening, my worst fear was confirmed by the PI. He had, in fact, gone to L.A. and was with another woman. That was the beginning of my life crashing down around me. I later found out that he had been cheating on me almost from the beginning, with various women including escorts.

My heart was completely broken, and I thought it couldn't get worse, but it did. By the time I finally was able to leave for good, he had become an emotionally abusive, narcissistic man that had no concern for me or his children. The last straw was during an argument when he threatened to bash my face in if I didn't shut up. I believed him and filed for divorce the following day.

At the age of 40, I left with nothing but my two boys ages two and four, my car, and few belongings. I had to start my life over from scratch.

Sometimes your dreams become nightmares, but thankfully that is not the end of the story...

I want to leave you with hope. In the last ten years, I have rebuilt my life one piece at a time. It was hard, but now I am living my true dream to help other women to live a life of freedom from toxic relationships, codependency, low self-esteem, anxiety, and depression – to show them that self-love is the key to attaining what we desire in life.

When we operate from that place, then we will attract higher vibrational people and situations into our lives and break free from the subconscious programming of the past.

When I got married, I thought I had achieved my dream of being a mom and wife. When that all came crashing down after finding out my husband was unfaithful, not only having an affair but also a sexual addiction to prostitutes, it made me wake up to what I had attracted in my life, based on my deep-rooted abandonment issues stemming from my parent's divorce.

At 40 years old, I had to pick up the pieces of my shattered dreams and the life I thought I was going to have and start over with two small kids in tow, one with special needs. I was broken and at my lowest point. I didn't know how I was going to survive.

I moved back in with my mother and did what I had to do to put food on the table. I bartended five nights a week and started my private practice back up.

Slowly, I started to put the pieces of my life back together. I took a deep dive into my own personal development, attending seminars, events, and taking online courses as often as I could. Within my own healing, I realized the greater need of the collective. I encountered so many beautiful souls on their own healing journey and wanted to impact the world in a larger way!

I decided to turn my pain into my purpose and created an online course to help other women who have been through the same types of things I did. Every day is a triumph as I equip others to live a life of freedom.

I want you to learn from my journey. The three lessons I want to leave with you are these:

- You were created wonderful and complete. You do not need a spouse in your life to be happy.
- Listen to that inner voice. It was put there as a way of protecting you from harm.
- You are never too old to start again and live a new dream. I am content in my own skin now, and it is incredible how free I feel. I can be myself and love myself for who I am. I now know that, "The future belongs to those who believe in the beauty of their dreams." (Eleanor Roosevelt).

Believe in yourself. Believe in your dreams and never let anyone tell you that you need someone else in your life to be complete!

Hillary Foster, MFT

Hillary Foster, MFT

Hillary Foster is a Licensed Marriage, Family & Relationship Therapist. For 19 years, she has helped people struggling with relationships, anxiety, and depression. She is passionate about empowering people to live a life of freedom!

If stress, anxiety, and fear are robbing you from enjoying your life, Hillary will help you identify your past traumas, current stressors, and limiting beliefs to help you re-write your story to create a life you love! She believes the most important relationship we have is with ourselves.

Hillary's ability to help clients stems from compassion, education, and experience. She holds a BA in Psychology from the University of Colorado and an MA in Psychology from Antioch University. She started her private practice in 2001 and during her 19 years as a therapist has seen what works when it comes to modifying behavior. Her approach is solution focused. She uses transformational therapeutic techniques to assist you in identifying the source that holds you back from achieving your desired goals.

If you want to enjoy life more and improve your relationships, you will benefit from working with Hillary Foster. She believes that when you connect your mind, body, and soul, the possibilities are endless.

www.hillaryfoster.com

CHAPTER 16

Secure Your Legacy
by Dr. Cheryl D. George

*H*ave you ever hit a stage in life where it was good, but you became unsatisfied and hungry for something new? That is the place that I found myself in 2008. I had a wonderful life in New York City with family, friends, a business, and church. However, there was a growing longing in my heart.

After much soul searching, I decided to leave NYC and move to Chicago. There was a pastor that I had become friends with, and I admired her relationship with God. I knew that I needed her to mentor me. The plan was to spend six months learning from this amazing woman and doing a joint venture with her on some business deals, and then progress to the next phase of my life.

Chicago was a big adjustment for me; the worst was the winter months. As a child, my mother would tell me that "This is for grown folks." Winters in Illinois are not to be played with. I was sick for the first four winters; yes, that was four in a row that Ole Man Winter prevailed. The last one knocked me off my feet and I found myself at the hospital in the intensive care unit with a machine plugged into my body. I had no health insurance, and the $67,000 hospital bill was fully my responsibility.

That hospital visit would be the beginning of a turning point for me, but I did not know it. All I could see was the bad. My favorite book (the Bible) tells us that "all things work together for our good," but when you are hurting, your pain can blind you to the truth. That is why I love hindsight – it always has perfect 20/20 vision.

During my hospital stay, there was one person that visited every day and sometimes twice a day for the nine days I was there. She would comb my hair, sing songs, and even cook for the nurses. Frances' devotion surprised me because although we were members of the same church, we did not spend a lot of time together. She was much younger than me, married, and a new mom.

She became the younger sister I never knew I wanted or needed, and I adopted her, her husband, and her beautiful babies as my own. I had no idea at the time, but Frances would lead me to my true calling.

The Event That Changed My Life

One year later, events would spiral me into a path that I never expected.

Frances was an inspiration to everyone she met. She was a young mother of toddler children who was happily married to a man 30 years her senior. They lived a happy and fulfilling life together as a loving family. Life was good.

Frances was a vibrant and joyful Caribbean girl from Jamaica. She was a wonderful cook and a devoted mother who enjoyed her work as a hairdresser. She led the choir at my church with love, talent, and patience.

When Frances sang for the congregation on a Sunday, she created an atmosphere of joy and healing that was a tribute to not only her lovely spirit but to the relationship she had with God, her family, and friends. Her talent was a gift to us all.

Sadly, Frances suffered a brain aneurysm shortly after her 29th birthday. She was hospitalized and had surgery, which seemed to have been successful.

During her recovery time in the hospital, she got out of bed without assistance and fell, striking her head, and that accident ultimately caused her tragic passing.

Frances' death shocked me and my church family to our core. There was a palpable void left at our worship services without her impactful and loving presence. Then I found out something that shook me to my inner most being, and it inspired a profound change in my life.

My Inspiration

I discovered that Frances did not have life insurance when she passed. Her husband was a taxi driver and he struggled to save enough to provide her with a proper burial. Frances was not laid to rest for many weeks after she died, and this compounded the tragedy.

Even though we did eventually have a funeral for her, I never felt like I got to say a proper goodbye. The grieving process was delayed, and it felt like there was no closure. She was my little sister and my heart hurt that we couldn't bury her sooner.

Frances' death and what happened afterward spurred me to study and acquire my insurance licenses. I was resolved that no other family should have to endure the pain of losing a loved one, and then having to wait to lay them to rest with dignity and in a timely fashion. Not to mention my own issue with the $67,000 medical bill hanging over my head.

I did not know which insurance I wanted to do, so I decided to do them all: property, casualty, life, and health. Eight exams in all and I was going to do it for my birthday in six weeks. Everyone thought I was nuts, including other insurance agents, my teachers, family, and friends.

They kept telling me, "You should do one or two and then come back." In my heart there was an urgency. I was in my late 40's, kissing 50, and there was no time to wait. I trusted that my determination and commitment to my new mission would get me through.

Lesson #1: Sometimes you have to go for your dreams alone.

Every day, I would pack a lunch, take my truck, and drive to a parking lot. With the windows down, my phone off, and my seat pushed back as far as it can go, I would study for four to six hours straight. Everyone thought I was in over my head, but that did not matter. I was driven by determination and the pain in my heart outweighed any obstacle.

Every year I do something major on my birthday and I had decided for that year my "thing" would be getting all the licenses on the first shot.

It took two full days to complete the exams. Property and casualty were four parts; I took those first. I could have gotten the results from the first four at the end of the day, but I wouldn't allow them to give them to me. I put the results away. I did not want the results to influence the rest of my exams.

For round two, I ate a great breakfast, all protein, and then took the life and health exams. By the time I finished the exams, all of my body was drained. When they told me that I passed all of the exams, my knees buckled!! Joy filled my body – I did it!!!! I did what they told me I could not do!

Lesson #2: It does not matter if no one did it before you; if you believe you can do it, then DO IT!!!

Part of the process of getting your licenses is being sponsored by an agent. So, when I came back to the office and walked in the door, I was so drained, he thought that I failed. When I handed him all the documents, he couldn't believe that I passed. He said, "You did something I could not do. I have been in insurance for 14 years and have not seen anybody take them all and pass on the first attempt."

Then I called my pastor and she really celebrated me. She took me out, and even told the church. When she did that, I said to myself, "I would never allow those licenses to expire even if I never sold another insurance policy because it was so hard and such a difficult achievement."

After working in property and casualty for a major carrier for 18 months, I moved to a large brokerage in downtown Chicago. Obamacare was starting up and they needed 1,000 agents to handle the load. Over the next four years, I was in the top five percent of agents in the company. When others were laid off during the slow season, I was made a permanent employee.

My mother's health was declining, so I resigned from the brokerage and started my own insurance company. This allowed me the flexibility to travel and work at the same time.

Don't Lose Your Dream

Insurance can be scary and complex. There are so many things that I did not know until I got into the industry. I wish it were taught in school along with finance. Without the proper coverage, anything you build can be lost by one illness, lawsuit, and/or death. I have seen and heard so many horror studies; each one breaks my heart because I believe that if people knew better, they would do better.

Did you know that more people insure their cell phones than they do their lives? It is true; 80 percent of cell phones have coverage versus 49 percent of people.

I recently had a car accident and was hit from behind. It was very scary. Once the police report was filed and it was time to call the insurance company, I was so relieved that the proper coverage was in place; everything was being taken care of. We do not have to have any additional stress in an already stressful situation. That is what insurance is: peace of mind when you need it.

My dream has become simply to help people live a good life here on Earth, then leave a legacy when they are gone. The best way to show your love is to make sure that those who are left behind have the best coverage possible.

I know of one situation where a client canceled her policy because she wanted to use the money for something else. One week later, she was gone, and the family was left not only grieving for their loved one, but financially trying to find a way to pay for everything.

Don't be that person. Be the brave one who understands that death comes to us all. Face it head-on by preparing ahead of time and providing well for those who are left behind.

My mission is going well. This path that I am on led me to here, writing this chapter for you. I have written over 2,000 polices and protect the lives of people that I will never meet. I smile when I think of the children, spouses, parents, and grandparents that are covered because someone loved them enough to plan for their future. I had a small hand in that, and it feels amazing…to God be the Glory. I would love to leave you with three thoughts:

- Insurance is not an expense; it is an investment in the future.
- When you become restless in life, it is time to look inward; there is a new dream developing.
- Don't be afraid to start your dream alone. When the time is right, others will join you.

I experience my dream life every day. I can't imagine how boring my life would be if I hadn't taken the risk and started something new. Now it is your turn!

Dr. Cheryl George

Dr. Cheryl D. George

Dr. Cheryl D. George embodies the spirit of pioneer women entrepreneurs. Since early adulthood, she has spent almost 25 years honing her business acumen by starting and/or helping over 200 small businesses and ministries.

Dr. George has received several acknowledgments, including the Caribbean American Chamber of Commerce and Industry for being an up-and-coming Under 40 Entrepreneur for her Exousia Business in 1994, and six years later, in 2000, the Female Entrepreneur of the Year by the Women's Venture Fund (WVF).

In 2003 she started a new company, SEED Financial, in New York, which focuses on the financial and investment services to organizations. Ms. George continues her entrepreneurial spirit with her most recent endeavor, Insure With Cheryl. Cheryl is a licensed Health and Life agent in all 50 states and handles IRAs, Mutual Funds, 401Ks, and other types of retirement funds. Cheryl is a lifelong learner, who transforms learning into economic opportunities and contributes generously to the business world, to society, and generously to her local community.

Connect with Cheryl at:
www.InsureWithCheryl.com
info@InsureWithCheryl.com

CHAPTER 17

Embrace Your Why
by *Cynthia Dales*

I absolutely hated going to the doctor because I had to step on that awful scale and find out what I weighed. I heard the nurse say 292 pounds and I wanted to die! The voice in my head said, "You are fat," as the doctor looked me in the eyes and said, "You need to lose weight. You also have high blood pressure and need to be on medication."

I was angry; I had eaten myself up to 292 pounds and was only in my 20's. I had tried many diets. I would lose weight, then yo-yo back up again. I had become a weight-loss expert and could have written a book on "how" to lose weight but couldn't figure out how to keep it off. Weight loss had become a nightmare carnival ride that never ceased to end. After so many failures, I finally gave up and decided I was doomed to be fat for the rest of my life.

After years of not caring about myself and being heavy, I decided that I needed a new focus in my life. I decided to go to school to become a teacher. By that time, I was 34 years old, weighed 278 pounds, worked full-time during the day, and went to school at night. Little did I know that I was going to get the shock of a lifetime that would change my life forever.

I wasn't feeling very well and wondered if I might be pregnant. A pregnancy would be a miracle due to my weight-related issues. I had also been told by a doctor when I got married that it would be "an act of God" if we had a child. I never in a million years thought I would have a child naturally, but, surprise, the test was positive.

During the pregnancy, I developed pre-eclampsia and gestational diabetes, and had to be hospitalized several times. The doctor put me on total bed rest for the last three months. The baby was healthy and doing fine, but me, not so much. The transition of coming to a screeching halt and laying on my side for three long months was brutal, but I knew I had to do it for the miracle of life that I was carrying. I felt I was going to lose my mind during that time, and the negative self-talk reared its ugly head repeatedly about my weight and how it hindered yet another thing in my life.

When the baby was born, I was so happy. I thought it would be the time to get my weight under control and maybe my life would finally be better. However, being a new mom and unemployed for almost a year caused stress and money issues, and, once again, my weight started to climb.

So there I was; my life was rolling by. I was still fat and now depressed, frustrated, and sick. Every year I would get on the New Year's resolution bandwagon and say, "This is the year I will lose weight and get healthy." I would start a diet and a few weeks or months into it, bam, some stress, crisis, or event would derail me again. Now I felt the added pressure of needing to get healthy since I was a parent and had a child to raise.

The evil weight-loss carnival ride continued for the next seven years as I watched the numbers on the scale go up and down. In 2008, I vowed to beat obesity once and for all and decided to join a gym and hire a personal trainer. I was really working hard and had reached the

210-pound range, was extremely motivated, and felt good about my progress.

In January 2009, we found out that my dad was sick; the final diagnosis was small cell lung cancer, and it was terminal. We were told that my dad didn't have long to live. He tried chemotherapy, but it didn't go well, and in the process, we found out he had a widow-maker – a 99 percent blockage in his heart.

I was scared and stressed, so I ate a lot. I knew every floor in the hospital that had vending machines with candy that I loved. One afternoon I went into my dad's hospital room while snacking, and he had such a sad look on his face. Even as sick as he was, he always greeted me with a big smile and a hug, but this day was different.

My dad typically was a very quiet man, and when he spoke, you listened because it was always something insightful. He said, "Honey, you have worked so hard to lose weight. Do me a favor and please don't let what is happening to me cause you to eat things you shouldn't." I threw the candy away, wanting to cry. I loved my dad so much, and he was right!

After a failed attempt at chemotherapy due to his bad heart, he went home with hospice care and fought like a warrior for 77 days. On his last day, when I saw him, I said, "Dad, it is okay to go home. I will take care of mom." I knew it worried him to leave her. Later that night he died, and I knew I had to get healthy to fulfill my promise that I made to him to be here to take care of my mom.

Struggling with my weight after the loss of my dad, it took another five years before I got brave and had gastric sleeve surgery. In 2014, I was 238 pounds and was scared but determined to win the weight battle and get off the carnival ride for good.

I did everything the doctor said and more. I worked hard and hit my goal weight of 150 pounds in nine months. Reaching my goal weight was like a dream. I was told by the doctors and nurses that I was a great success story.

About a year after surgery, the marketing people for the bariatric group asked me to do a photoshoot for newspaper ads, to be the subject of a magazine article, to go to a Phoenix Suns game and be recognized for my accomplishments, and to run a five kilometer race. I clearly remember the morning of the race; there were thousands of people watching and running. I heard my internal voice say, "What are you doing here? You can't do this!" I was surprised that the nagging self-talk was still giving me grief, even after losing all the weight and all I had accomplished.

I heard the gun go off, and I started running. I felt pretty good during the first half mile or so, then I started to alternate walking and running. The runners had thinned out, and I pushed myself hard to keep going. When I saw mile marker two, my inner voice said, "Hey, I am over halfway and not dead yet!" I was getting tired, my lungs hurt, and I was discouraged with my pace, but I kept going.

Coming around a bend, I slowed to a race walk, and when I looked up, there was a huge anchor as a Navy memorial. I stopped in front of it, saluted, and began to tear up. I knew in my heart that my dad was there with me! Both of my parents were in the Navy, and their service meant the world to them.

Suddenly, I felt an intense burst of energy and ran like the wind. As I saw the finish line and crossed it, I started to cry. I finally knew my dad was proud of what I had accomplished by getting to my goal and becoming healthy, and so was I.

Even though I had someone in my life who was my biggest cheerleader and supporter, I needed to learn to love myself enough to make a transformation. It took losing my dad and getting told that I was pre-diabetic to figure out what I needed to change for good. This is when I found my "Why." I knew I had to lose the weight to fulfill my promise to him and to myself.

Once I hit my goal and really owned it, it made me realize that we all have greatness to offer this world, and if we aren't doing something with it while we are here on this earth, we are being selfish and depriving the world of what we have to offer. This was when my "real" transformation began, and I recognized that the weight is what had been holding me back the whole time.

I now understand that I have been on this journey all of my life to share my story to inspire you and let you know your dreams are possible if you face your fears, take a leap, believe in yourself, and go for it!

Obesity is a terrible disease that robs you of who you are supposed to be. The diet and exercise are fairly easy; the truly hard part of this journey is "uncovering" your why, the actual reason(s) for wanting to change your life and transform. You must figure out what is holding you back from doing this for yourself, and what will propel you to greater health so you can give your gift to the world.

Losing the weight was the beginning for me, and as I continued to learn about loving myself and who I was becoming, I started to dream about one day becoming a certified fitness trainer. I wanted to work with pre- and post-op bariatric clients to help them be successful in losing their weight and achieving their goals.

I had an opportunity to meet some amazing people at a conference who motivated me to make my dream come true. I knew in my heart that I had something I needed to say and desperately wanted to help others, which fueled me even more, so I started researching, learning, and educating myself.

These actions led to a very powerful big step, and I recently became a certified fitness trainer. I am taking another step and working on my transformation specialist certification so I can also help people with the mental side of living a healthy and happy life!

After all of these blessings, this amazing opportunity came to me, allowing me to write and share my story to let the world know about my transformational journey, how it impacted my life, and how it allowed me to be able to start living and owning my dreams. During my journey, there has been a lot of self-discovery as a result of freeing myself from all the extra weight and baggage I carried around for so many years.

I learned that I must love myself, continue working on stopping the negative self-talk, and take care of myself first before I try to care for others. That is exactly what we as obese people need to learn to do: put ourselves first, learn to love ourselves, and take care of our health before we take care of others.

So, you might be wondering why I titled this chapter Embrace Your Why! After my weight-loss surgery, I walked every day, and I started noticing when I was outside that there were lots of butterflies; I knew they were somehow important in this process.

I want you to keep something in mind as you start your transformation: caterpillars must go through a lot of hard work to get out of that cocoon to become a butterfly, and if someone does it for them, they don't come out of the process correctly. I want you to understand that this might be hard, but trust me, the work that you put in will be worth the reward of spreading your wings and showing the world the beautiful butterfly that you are!

Now that I have shared my transformation, you may be inspired and want to know where to begin? Here are a few things I have learned:

- First, you will need to admit you have an unhealthy relationship with food. Please be aware that my surgery did not "cure" this issue; it is only a tool to help with weight loss. The food relationship/addiction is real and is something that will need to be worked on daily.

- Next, you must figure out your reason for wanting this change, your "Why?"
- Most important, educate yourself about what your weight loss options are, and which are right for you. Speak with your doctor and enlist him/her as an advocate. Gastric sleeve surgery was the tool I used for my weight loss, but this may not be right for you. Therefore, I strongly encourage you to educate yourself and consult with a medical professional.

No matter where you are at in your healthy living journey, these tips will help you:

- Be mindful when eating and enjoy your food, the company, and your surroundings.
- Before eating, ask yourself, are you hungry? Are you making a nutritious choice versus a quick emotional fix?
- Make your meals at least half fruit and vegetables.
- Drink lots of water!
- Have a "treat" occasionally to keep from losing your mind (unless this is a slippery slope for you). Change your thinking patterns from good and bad foods to nutritious and not as nutritious foods; it will make a difference in the choices you make.
- Log or track your food to stay on course.
- Exercise the way you love best! This will help you stick to it and keep it from being a chore.
- Lower stress by having fun!
- Take 30-minute electronics breaks before bed and when you wake up. (Give your brain a chance to decompress.)
- Take time every day to be grateful, see things more positively, and be kind to yourself. (Take time for self-care!)

I strive to incorporate these healthy living tips into my life daily. Living this way has helped me to continue to stay at a healthy weight and have a positive outlook on life. I can do things I was never able to before and give back for the blessings I have received. I have run many five and eight km runs for charity events and helped reroof a house for Habitat for Humanity.

Please remember your "why" for wanting to transform. You are a very special person, and I believe in you! You truly have so much to offer, and there is a big world out there just waiting for you. There is an old saying, "You don't waste good." You are good; heck, better than good, you are amazing! Some days will be tough. However, the freedom of living a balanced life and the joy that goes with it is priceless. When you reach your goal, you will feel the strength and peace that comes from your accomplishment of becoming healthy and being the beautiful butterfly that you are! Now, embrace your "why," then spread your wings, fly, and own your dreams!

Cynthia Dales

Cynthia Dales

Cynthia Eggleston Dales is an ISSA-certified fitness trainer and transformation specialist. Cynthia has been on a five-year journey, becoming a master at transforming and feeding the mind as well as the body.

Her proudest achievements are having a child, achieving her weight loss goal, and maintaining it for over five years, and becoming a personal trainer and author.

She loves to help others realize they are worthy of reaching their health goals by helping them build their self-confidence and learning to love themselves enough to make healthy choices with their food and exercise.

She currently trains clients in Gilbert, Arizona and is a Business Manager at a Lutheran Church in Chandler, AZ. She started a new project in the Fall of 2019, creating online fitness training courses for pre- and post-operative bariatric patients.

You may learn more about Cynthia's journey and services at www.cynthiadales.com or get inspirational weight loss motivation on Instagram @cldales.

CHAPTER 18

Master Your Money
by Haziq Ali

*I*t's hard to learn from winning, especially when you had a lot so young. My first taste of achievement was at the age of eleven when my first business did very well financially. I was celebrated on 60 Minutes, a national television show and became a pre-teen celebrity with the coins rolling in.

I was having fun, but there was no one telling me what to do with the money. My family tried to guide me, but advice from family can often lead a person to do the opposite and rebel, and that is what I did.

I felt justified in my unwise actions, but I never realized that if you do it long enough, that's now your new habit! Our habits form our future, and mine became filled with misguided business decisions that left my businesses in a state of feast or famine, all or nothing.

My attitude towards money became reckless because I always felt like there was more of it coming. It didn't stop at money; my attitude transferred into many other areas of my life. Like Bill Gates said, "Success is a lousy teacher."

My big dreams were coming to life. I was married and building a family with my beautiful wife, helping fund a record label, and reconciling with my entrepreneur father. While not realizing that I lacked a foundation, the element necessary for any structure to be stable, my world soon started to crumble.

My wife and I ended up in a bitter divorce, where it felt like I left with nothing, including my soul. My vegetarian, non-drinking, non-smoking father suddenly died of cancer, just as we were getting close for the first time.

To top it off, an employee I had helped got caught doing an illegal activity that resulted in all of my retail stores being raided during the Christmas shopping season. The charges were eventually dropped, but not before causing me bankruptcy, foreclosure, and homelessness, along with thoughts of suicide.

I couldn't understand why, after working so hard, for so long and generating well over seven figures, I had absolutely nothing to show for it. What had I missed? What should I have done differently? If I was supposed to be so smart, how did all these things happen to me? Asking these very important questions opened my mind to a new level of self-awareness.

My father's death also had an unusual effect on me. As I reflected on his life, all the lessons that he taught me came back. I was learning from him all over again, and I knew that I couldn't quit. I realized that having won and lost, I could start over, and this time learn how to do things the right way.

The first was an event company that specialized in award ceremonies. It grew so fast, and one of the events we did became so popular with celebrities that one of the major celebrity award companies sent us a cease and desist order. That was the end of that business. Through it, I learned that you might have a great idea, but if you grow too fast, others can get jealous and try to sabotage you.

It couldn't stop me as I started a different business. There came the point when I knew that it was time to move on to the next one.

Each business taught me lessons that I applied to the next one, and now I can truly say that I am a successful entrepreneur.

As Dr. Ona says, "I share this not to impress you, but to impress upon you that awareness is powerful." It is the difference between staying the same and deciding to change. It is awareness that brought me to the point of change, not the pain.

Many entrepreneurs try, fail, and give up. Not me. Success is determined by what you do after failure. Those lessons from my dad caused an inner awareness that gave me the courage to try again when all I wanted to do was give up.

In this chapter, I'm going to share with you the knowledge that I wished I knew before I started my adult entrepreneurial journey. Soak this information in and allow it to increase your awareness to a level that will make staying the same hard for you (although you'll try because the "comfort zone" is a master of seduction). Once you understand what the rules are, you can win if you master them with repetition.

The Lessons I Learned

1. Your Future Lifestyle Must Be Handled by Investments.

A simple objective that most never get to. Dave Ramsey of Financial Peace University released a study that says that 58% of Americans don't have $1000 saved for a crisis. How many people do you know who have six months of income saved? Or are they paying this month's bills with this month's money?

What's stopping us? Believe it or not, the best thing going for us is also the worst thing against us: we live in the type of economic system we call capitalism, and capitalism depends on ignorance. For example, why do we pay a barber or hairdresser for a haircut? They know something that we don't.

People shop at Walmart because Walmart knows something they don't: where to buy milk cheaper so they can make a bigger profit. No one's going to step into Walmart and say, "Now wait a minute. Why are you selling that flat-screen television for $800 when you only paid $25 for it in China?" Instead, if I'm willing to pay for it, they're allowed to sell it. Clearly, capitalism is based on ignorance.

2. Capitalism Is Not Your Friend!

The good news is that if capitalism is based on ignorance, if you learn more, you earn more! The bad news is that ignorance spreads, and therefore, so does poverty. Two different institutions noticed this and decided to do something about it: corporations and the government.

Before the industrial revolution, America was 80 percent entrepreneurs and only 20 percent workers. When someone approached an entrepreneur and asked him to work for them, they'd say, "You're trying to trick me into working for you! I can't pass that job down to my children, so why would I do that?"

Now, people act as though working a job is one of the ten commandments: "Thou shalt work 40 hours per week." That wasn't God's plan; that was Henry Ford's! He said, "I know you're used to working sunup to sundown, but here you only have to work 40 hours a week!" Thus began the idea of "employee benefits."

Soon, workers became widespread, and businesses needed to step it up to attract talent. They began to offer pensions, saying, "If you work for me for 30 years, I'll take care of you for another 30 years."

When your parents gave you the classic advice, "Get a good job with good benefits," it wasn't horrible; it's just now outdated. I imagine it was also wise at one time to carry quarters in case you needed to make a phone call. Times change, and we have to adjust and adapt.

The other institution that came to the "rescue" is the government. When it became apparent that these companies were still leaving many out in the cold, and our aging, poor society was in danger of embarrassing us on the world stage, guess who tried to adapt first? The government.

Franklin Delano Roosevelt's administration saw that nobody had money to retire and came up with Social Security, which is designed to help people retire gracefully when labor was no longer an option. Unfortunately, it was intended for the "outliers" or exceptions to the rule: those who lived longer. Back then, people didn't live much past the age of 65.

Now the majority live well beyond that, and social security was never designed to support them all. It's become a "Ponzi scheme" where the money is taken from the working people in their prime and given to the retirees while telling those workers how great their investment is working out.

Many experts say that if you are 45 or younger, you're never going to see social security in your retirement. Doesn't that change the way you need to play the game?

So why is everyone struggling if this is the wealthiest country in the world? I'll give you five legitimate reasons:

➢ **Inflation.** Inflation, the invisible income killer, is why I say, "Savers are losers." When President Nixon took us off the "gold standard", our cash became a device designed to keep our money in savings even when the marketplace kept moving. Think about Grandma back in the day and all that she could buy for $.35, even a full meal. If she had "saved" that money under her pillow or put it in a low-interest savings account, today she couldn't even buy a cup of coffee.

Paper money "stills" your wealth while inflation invisibly reduces its value. For example, when the price of gas goes up, farmers charge more for their crops to pay for their equipment, the distributor charges the grocery store more, and the grocery store charges the consumer more. If you go to your boss and ask for a raise because gas and food prices have risen, do you think you'll get an increase in your pay? Not likely. When a business owner's costs rise, they can raise their prices; but when a worker's costs rise, all they can raise...is their blood pressure.

➢ **Taxes.** On average, workers pay 30 percent of their income to taxes.

The founding fathers were entrepreneurs and investors who set up the country for people like them. If you gross $50,000 at your job and bring home $35,000 after taxes versus if you profit $50,000 from the sale of your home, and you are taxed much less on that profit, wouldn't you be better off investing in property?

Inflation and taxation are both reasons to create a business; the former because you control the profit, the latter because, especially with the 2017 tax law that favors businesses, you need a business to avoid seeing your income stripped at an even higher rate.

The first two reasons are responsible for the third...

➢ **Debt.** Debt is an effect of taxes. For example, if you go to the bank to get a loan, they loan you money based on your net income, not your gross, even though the difference is being paid to taxes. The bank is lending you money they know you can't pay back. They set the loan up, so you lose. Why?

Remember: capitalism depends on ignorance. With inflation, businesses exist to make money. For taxes, the government makes money. So, with debt, it's the banks making money.

The fourth reason? You were born in the "U.S.A."

➢ **That is, the United States of Advertising.** Big businesses spend billions of dollars each year on schemes to remove money from your bank account. Take Amazon. They do research where subjects are attached to electrodes that monitor what happens in the customer's brain as they walk through a warehouse. Why? Because our society is built on consumption. There is something every month designed to rob you of your chances for financial freedom.

Let's not forget all of the weddings, anniversaries, birthdays, funerals, prom, graduations, etc. That's interesting, but more so, it's intentional.

The final reason is especially insidious in the urban community.

➢ **Self-image.** Why can't we have regular sneakers instead of Air Jordans? Why do ladies go to a salon instead of getting nail polish at the store? The insecurity about how what you buy defines who you are is amplified by industries worldwide. Having a new car every year or new furniture every two years, it's all rooted in self-image. Beware, it will make you broke.

How Do You Fight Capitalism?

What's the prescription for this middle-class sickness? Despite these legitimate reasons for failure, there are three simple steps to success.

➢ **Cash Flow Management.** While the poor measure money with dollars, the wealthy measure their money with…time. For example, if I'm a basketball player making a million dollars a year, but I go to the same club and buy the same car as someone making ten million, is that going to work well for me? If I make a million dollars per year, but I spend two million, I have only six months of cash flow because you measure it in time.

Let's say I'm a teacher who makes $70,000 per year, but I only spend $35,000; I have two years of cash flow, and I'm doing better than that guy making a million a year and spending two million!

Your first goal is to get to positive cash flow. What's the difference? Positive cash flow is when an abundance of cash saves or makes you money. Negative cash flow is when a lack of money costs you money. For example, if you buy a car that lists for $20,000, but they take your offer of $15,000 in cash, you just saved $5,000. On the other hand, if you have to take a loan out and pay interest in fees, you are paying up to $30,000 for the same car.

To improve your cash flow:

- lower your taxes
- minimize your expenses
- eliminate your debt
- increase your credit score
- accelerate your income

One crucial way to get to positive cash flow is to own a business on the side. You can legally play the system that has been set up in our country when you own a business.

➤ **Create business income.** The number to know for living a fulfilled life is what I call the "freedom now" number. Here's how it works...

Add up your monthly expenses plus what you need for entertainment and maybe your monthly travel fund. Whatever that number is, you will need that to come in residually, and you're free! One sure-fire way to create this level of business income (or even greater) is to find a crisis, stand in the middle of it, and serve in the most significant way possible.

What do the wealthy do with the extra money after the first two steps are complete?

➢ **Invest.** The reason I say "savers are losers" is not due to character or success level, but because of the idea that inflation "takes" at a faster rate than your savings account "gives." You have to put your money on top of something that's growing, or your money is dying.

Investing is an art that can be learned; remember, the more you learn, the more you'll earn.

I encourage you to surround yourself with stronger people. We are all a direct reflection of the expectations of our peer group. You are the average of the five people you hang around with the most. As my mom said, "If you hang with nine broke friends, you're bound to be the tenth!"

Remember, either your mind has to expand to match your goals or your goals will start to shrink to match your mind. Realizing massive success doesn't take you being special; it just requires you to do something special.

Owning your dreams is hard work, but the rewards are worth it. Don't be afraid to make the best investment you can; in yourself. As you do, awareness will grow, and soon you will be the master of your money instead of it mastering you.

Haziq Ali

Haziq Ali

A serial entrepreneur who was featured on 60 Minutes for his first business while still in junior high school, Haziq Ali has virtually never had a job.

After some huge learning experiences that left him divorced, bankrupt, foreclosed, and homeless, he applied the life-changing lessons he teaches to his own world. In the next 18 months he was able to open multiple businesses and generate substantial income, but most importantly, fall deeply in love with his life.

As a true believer that the best part of every man, woman, and child on the planet is the entrepreneur portion, in 2014 he helped to found Novae Money - a financial empowerment company focused on helping to support the economic lives of our community through personal development, financial literacy, and personal/ business credit & lending services.

Now in extremely high demand as a speaker and trainer plus TV/radio show guest, this author and entrepreneur literacy expert has been trained by the best. Using the same Nobel Peace prize nominated "accelerated-learning techniques" revered by Tony Robbins and many more, this high-impact servant has dedicated his life to transforming lives.

www.novaemoney.com

CHAPTER 19

Press Forward
by Charles Tchoreret

*W*hen you are young, your dreams are based on what you're going to do in life; when you are older, they switch to who you want to become. I have been very blessed in life to have both of those dreams come true for me, mostly because of a mother who taught me that anyone could succeed if they are willing to work hard enough at it.

When I was a secondary school student, math was not my favorite subject and it showed in my poor marks. My excuses fell on deaf ears with my mother; she told me that education is the key to open doors in society and that every subject in school counted. Mom helped me at times with homework, but she also told me to take full responsibility for my success – and failures – in life. Whenever negativity took control, she would pull me aside, sit me down, and help me see the other side of the coin.

As I began to take math more seriously, I finally understood that complaining about a situation and having negative thoughts was not the solution. I started to improve in math when I adopted a more positive attitude. When I went through moments of discouragement, my mom would sit me down and tell me to focus on success. She believed that everything is possible for those who believe.

Like most young adults, I imagined that "dream job," the one that would make my life complete. It was working for Shell Oil. It filled my thoughts, and I could see myself there working and travelling internationally. I could hear the sound of the plane revving up its engines, getting ready to take off. I could smell the ocean as I went to exotic places, and I could see myself in that expensive suit shaking hands with top managers, executives, and CEOs.

There was a problem; very few people my age got those kinds of positions without already knowing someone in the company. So I did the best I could, I got a job with British Gas, and I learned the ropes. When I was discouraged, I would remember what my mother taught me. She believed that everything happens for a reason, and it is up to each individual to learn from the experience. My focus was on learning what I needed to take that next step.

Finally, the time came to apply for the big job, and all of a sudden, I was overwhelmed with fear to the point that I convinced myself not to send in my cover letter and resume. I knew the procedure and what was needed, but I lacked the courage to take that leap of faith. Everyone in my family told me it was impossible, except my mom. She told me to go for it. Despite her support, I still dreaded the humiliation and fear failure would bring.

Mom was my strongest supporter throughout the process. From a young age, she always encouraged me to believe in myself and the One who makes all things possible. She prayed and encouraged me to pray as well. Her words strengthened my belief in myself. She would say things like, "You are as good as any other candidate, and I have no doubt that you will be recruited." At the time, I thought if Mom says so, it must be true, and I sent in my application.

She was right! Not only did I get the job, but I spent 25 amazing years working for this global corporation. It was my first career dream that came true. Besides marrying my soulmate and the birth of my four children, it was one of the most fulfilling moments I had ever experienced. I learned that nothing is impossible, and sometimes, the most significant results come from not being afraid to take those smaller actions.

What actions have you been putting off because you questioned if you would get any results? Is there a phone call you need to make or email that you need to send? Whatever it is, I encourage you to take that step of faith and do it. You never know when the opportunity will be gone. The time to take action is now.

Handling the Unexpected

When I was 28, I returned home to spend quality time with my family. My dad was traveling abroad for work and was due back home the following week. As Mom and I sat down for breakfast on that beautiful Sunday morning, the phone rang. She answered, and within a matter of seconds, she screamed, dropped the phone, and collapsed on a nearby chair.

I rushed to her side, wondering what was wrong, knowing that it was serious. She couldn't speak. She was not the sort of person to be easily overwhelmed by a situation, but at that moment, she looked like a boxer who had just been knocked out by a devastating blow.

I held her in my arms and repeatedly asked her what was wrong. In a moment of lucidity, she regained her composure and asked me, with a sense of urgency, to join her in prayer. She knew that she had to tap into something bigger than her strength to pull out of the potentially destructive emotions she was facing. As we held hands, she told me that Dad had passed away from a severe brain hemorrhage. I was devastated. My father was only 56 years old, and my mother, 46. At such a young age, she became a widow.

Despite her desperate attempt to appear strong, she was deeply in shock. Later, after friends and family began pouring into her house to be with us, she looked at me straight in the eyes, as if she had been re-energized by the moment of prayer we had, held my hands, and said, "Remember what I told you about the twists and turns of life? Well, this is one of them. I have to trust God to see me through this one, and what is coming."

I held her in my arms and told her, "You will be just fine, Mom," a cliché affirmation that I voiced without having a clue of what was going on inside of her and how she would cope. At that moment, I could not imagine the uphill emotional struggles she would face.

Ultimately, my mom knew at that point that the battle had just started. She knew that she had to stand up and walk again. Like the great Les Brown said, "When life knocks you down, try to land on your back; because if you can look up, you can get up. Let your reason get you back up." That is what she did. She refused to be overwhelmed by her predicament and drown in the deep ocean of emotions.

Despite my age and professional experience, my father's death changed me. His death was like losing a part of me. The fact that he died overseas added to the shock, numbness, denial, and anger that started invading my mind. I never had a chance to tell my dad how much he meant to me and to say goodbye. Crippling emotions stayed with me for months, and I knew I had to pull out of them, for both my sake and my mom's. However, she appeared emotionally stronger than me and seemed to manage her grief very well. She was the one consoling me.

My parents loved each other deeply, and their relationship was so strong that they were often referred to as the perfect couple, even though they knew that their marriage, just like all marriages, was far from being perfect. They knew that to keep that flame burning brighter every day, despite the inevitable challenges, they had to put God in the center of it all, which they did so well!

One explanation for their long-lasting "love affair" is the fact that Mom was not trying to find a "soulmate" or someone who would complete her. Looking for someone to complete her was, spiritually speaking, idolatry. She had to find her fulfillment and purpose in God. My dad, just like her, had bad days.

They sometimes yelled at each other or were sometimes selfish. Despite these imperfections, she knew that God brought them together to steer each other in His direction. She told me once that every time they were going through some rocky path in their marriage, she would pray this prayer: Lord, how can I love my husband today like he's never been loved and never will be loved?

One day, as we were having a discussion, she told me something that helped me a great deal many years later. She said, "I lost your dad, and I feel sad and lonely. Yes, I have you, and I'm grateful for your support. One thing I want you to remember is that everything we hold sacred falls down one day, never to be mended. However, death is not the end."

Then, she told me the analogy of the train of life. "We are all passengers of that train from the time we are born. Along the journey, some significant people will board the train with you: siblings, friends, and even the love of your life. Your father stepped out of the train at a time and a designated station, leaving a permanent vacuum in my heart.

"Our ride together was one of joy, challenges, expectations, and finally, farewell. The success of your journey will depend on the kind of relationship you will develop with all passengers of the train, and how you will decide to lead your life. The mystery is that not a single passenger on the train knows when or at which station he or she will step off. Therefore, each passenger is responsible for giving the best of himself throughout the journey and leaving behind good memories of who he or she was. That is how to build your legacy." That powerful lesson blew my mind. At that moment, I not only knew that I would be okay, but I committed myself to make all the relationships in my life matter.

My mom's dream life had suddenly come to an end, and yet she was able to go on. She knew that when the time was right, another dream would appear. Eventually, dreams die, but there is always a new one to be found if you chose to open up your heart and dream again.

One of the things I learned from watching my mother go through the pain of losing her husband, was just how short life is and the importance of cherishing each day we are blessed with, which led me to do a lot of self-reflection. In doing so, I realized that I was living out a dream that I had as a child, but had not considered the dream of my heart as an adult man.

A Time for Change

That led me to realize that working a job was no longer my dream. I had more in me than just going to work every day and coming home. It wasn't that I didn't enjoy what I do, but there was a restlessness inside of me for something more.

As I thought about it, I knew that I wanted to start my own business, helping others awaken the greatness inside of themselves. Working for one of the top oil companies in the world taught me a lot. I would say that it was my playground for the entrepreneur life I have today. Learning about different cultures, traveling to over 20 different countries on five continents forged my personality into a forward-looking and dynamic individual who is comfortable in any environment or crowd.

My life is filled with opportunities to make a difference and help others. This is what I love to do.

Making Your Dreams Come True

The lessons I learned from my mother instilled in me from a young age – the mindset and skills I needed to succeed in life and live my dreams. My mom is in heaven now, but she will live on in me, her grandchildren, and now you. If you can remember the principles she taught me, you will not only be on the road to making your dreams come true, but it will honor her heart to see everyone be the greatest they can be.

Hard work is your friend and will create the momentum you need to propel you forward.

Education is the key to success. If you don't know how to do something – LEARN IT.

Every dream has its season, and when that season is over, it is time to find a new dream to go after.

Sometimes you know that it is time to move on, and then sometimes life moves on you. The end of one dream is never the end; it is only one door closing so that other doors may open.

It is time for the greatness in you to be unleashed. Find your dream and then make it happen as if your life depends upon it… Because it does.

Charles Tchoreret

Charles Tchoreret

Charles Tchoreret is an experienced supply chain management professional and an SAP Materials Management (MM) Consultant who worked 25 years in the oil and gas industry. He holds a bachelor's degree in applied language study from the University of North London, UK, and a master's degree in supply chain management from the University of Leicester, UK.

His job gave him the opportunity to live and work with his family in Holland, Europe, Nigeria, West Africa, and in Gabon, Central Africa. During his career, he traveled to four continents and visited over 50 different countries around the world. He is the proud father of three adult children and one teenager. He also has six grandchildren.

Charles is an international speaker, author, teacher, and coach who has dedicated his life to helping others reach their highest potential. He does this through entrepreneurship training and personal development coaching. His techniques allow you to accomplish more than you thought possible.

If you would like to find out more about working with Charles, please email him at tca@tcaconsultantsca.com.

CHAPTER 20

Travel Light
by Jennifer Evans

s a young girl, I remember daydreaming of going to Africa and helping people in need. As I grew up, that dream became distant. I was influenced by society and did what I was "supposed to," go to college, get a good job, and get married. Sound familiar?

From the outside, my life looked solid, but when I turned 26, the walls of my life collapsed. I found myself divorced, out of a job, and living back at my mom's house in Arizona.

I was embarrassed and felt like a failure, yet I still had hope for the future. I sought help, and after working closely with two life coaches, I landed back on my feet in the corporate world. I felt fortunate but unfulfilled, and my childhood dream to serve and travel began to reoccupy my mind. I believed deep down that my life was meant for something more.

I decided to put my dream to paper and wrote in my journal, "I have a calling from my soul, and I am planning the risk, leap, and jump of a lifetime! To leave it all for a service mission and personal journey of discovery and fun around the world, or at least to Europe!"

Against the sound judgment of close friends and family, I took that leap. I resigned from my job with no extra cash in the bank and no clue how this dream would become a reality.

On my last day on the job, I worked at a charity gala. Around midnight when the evening was winding down, I took a break alone on a bench. As I was scrolling through social media on my phone, I heard footsteps walking past me. I looked up, and to my surprise, it was the event honorees, renowned global philanthropists.

I was speechless. This husband and wife duo were living my dream! They had committed their lives to service and spent the majority of their time in third world countries, fitting people in need with hearing aids.

I said to myself, "Could this be my opportunity?"

Then thoughts of doubt crossed my mind, "No... I don't know what to say, and even if I did, they probably don't care what I have to say," but the deep desire inside of me outweighed the fear, and I jumped off the bench and ran up from behind them while politely calling their names. They stopped and turned around. As it turned out, they did care what I had to say, and my courage and genuine desire to serve made a favorable impression.

My dream was manifested. In April, 2012, I landed in Ethiopia, my first of 18 trips serving on the beautiful continent of Africa! Our mission was to spread peace and understanding around the world, and making people hear was the vehicle.

Imagine how you would feel witnessing someone hear for the first time or helping restore a grandmother's hearing after years of silence. My heart has softened to the sight of tough men crying, women dancing, and children giggling at the sound of their voices.

I began to help build and eventually scale community-based hearing healthcare programs in 45 countries throughout Latin America, Africa, the Middle East, Southeast Asia, and the Pacific.

I also had personal journeys of discovery and fun such as: boating the Amazon in Peru, witnessing the Dalai Lama deliver a sermon to 10,000 monks, dancing with tribal members in Papua New Guinea, floating in the Dead Sea, wildlife safaris in Tanzania, exploring ancient Petra in Jordan, snorkeling over the coral reef in Malaysia, trekking with silverback gorillas in Rwanda, and walking the streets of Bethlehem in Palestine. The list goes on and on with a grateful heart.

Best of all, I belonged to a mission team, a global family, and our efforts were impacting thousands of lives annually. We were road warriors serving overseas over 200 days per year: countless flights, hotel rooms, and rotary club dinners. My life was strenuous, but I loved it. I owned my dream.

Or did I?

Over time, my mental and physical health diminished. Chronic stress and jet lag took its toll. I was emotionally depressed and physically exhausted. Life on the road and the demands of my job played a factor, but there was a bigger issue that needed to surface...

The Secret Came Out

The first time I got drunk, I was 13 years old. I loved the feeling and wanted more. Throughout my teens and 20's, I was a "weekend warrior" partying hard on the weekends, yet somehow managing to be successful in school and work. My partying included excessive binge drinking accompanied by bad decisions and blackouts, and eventually marijuana, opioids, ecstasy, cocaine, meth, and psychedelics. I was a highly functioning addict.

However, when I was blessed to be part of that great mission, I knew it was time to cut back on the partying. My solution? Marijuana.

Smoking marijuana had been my favorite pastime for many years, but when the depression and exhaustion crept in, my use significantly increased to multiple times a day. Getting high made me feel better and escape the stress and my overactive mind.

Weed became "my medicine" that I needed daily and I put myself and our team at risk by smuggling it across borders around the world. My existence became solely about work and getting high, and not necessarily in that order.

For a few years, this lifestyle worked for me, but in the summer of 2016, I completely burnt out. Instead of going to my employer for help, I made a hasty decision and resigned from my job. I didn't know what was next, but I knew it was time for a change.

"I am a strong woman," I thought. "I can do this."

It was the longest month of my life, but I managed to stay marijuana-free for 30 days. I was proud of myself for having it "under control", so I decided it would be okay if I let myself get high once per week. I chose Sundays. I was able to manage this schedule for a month, and then I planned a trip home for the holidays.

Within days of returning to my old stomping grounds, I was back to getting high every few hours and enjoying countless cocktails on Saturday night with friends.

On one such morning after partying the night before, I woke up with a pounding headache and regretted not sticking to my self-imposed two-drink limit. I would have loved to lie in bed all day nursing my horrible cocaine hangover, but I had committed to taking my grandma to church.

I reluctantly pulled myself out of bed, got high, and picked up my grandma. As we walked into the church, I was handed the program for the service. I looked down at the paper, and the headline popped out at me like lightning illuminating the sky: "Addiction Must Fall."

I was stunned and did a double take. I mean, I believed in God, but this was different. He was talking to me.

I wish I could say I stopped drinking and doing drugs that day, but I was not able to. I felt like a hamster running in a wheel. I would wake up every morning and tell myself that I wouldn't get high that day, but my mind was consumed with desire, and by the time the evening came, I gave in. I didn't want to live this way anymore, but I could not stop.

I researched rehab facilities but could not afford one. I was able to get a coach. After a month of trying and failing at moderating myself, my mentor asked me if I had tried asking God for help.

"No," I said. "Why would I?"

I always had successfully relied on myself, but at this point, nothing I was doing was working, and I was desperate, so I gave it a try. I remember that night like it was yesterday. I knelt on my knees and prayed for the first time in many years. I told God that I was struggling and asked Him to help me change my story before something bad happened.

Soon after, I felt a nudge to look for support in my area, and then I made my way to my first 12-step meeting. Let me assure you; I did not want to be there. I thought, "I am not an alcoholic or addict like these people!" I was very tempted to walk away and never go back, but then I met a 60-year-old woman named Wendy. Her story reminded me of my own, and she had what I wanted - freedom from the bondage of addiction.

Wendy told me that if I wanted something I never had, then I needed to do something that I had never done before. I reluctantly took her suggestion and began to work the program. To my astonishment, my mental obsession and physical compulsion to use drugs and alcohol were removed. I experienced my miracle breakthrough.

My journey of recovery began. I floated on a pink cloud for a minute, and then reality set in. For the first time as an adult, I was feeling every emotion.

It was painful, but I knew there was nothing left for me in my old lifestyle, so I persevered. Yoga, 12-step meetings, and fellowshipping with other like-minded people helped me pull through.

Newly sober but still depressed, I attended a women's leadership meeting in Texas. I was the youngest of 12 women present. The other 11 appeared to be filled with joy and peace. I wondered what their formula was because I knew they weren't high on drugs. What I soon discovered was that they were women of faith and were high on the Holy Spirit.

Sound crazy? Well, it did to me! I grew up Catholic and always thought the Bible was a great reference book, though I never read it myself. I was a "spiritual person" and thought people that believed in Jesus were naïve. After spending time with these spirit-filled women, I began to wonder if Jesus was real, and was encouraged to ask questions.

The Bible says in Matthew 7:7, "Ask, and you shall receive, seek, and you shall find, knock, and the door will be opened." So that is exactly what I did. I opened my heart to the possibilities and talked to this so-called Jesus guy, "If you are real, please reveal yourself to me."

To my amazement, Jesus did reveal himself to me. He began speaking through what I call "uncoincidental" situations, communicating through people and scriptures to give me a personal knowledge of His truth and nearness.

The first time was in April 2017. I was on a flight to Dublin. It was like God spoke directly to me through the woman sitting across the aisle from me. As I continued to pursue Him, many more supernatural experiences happened and convicted me. So much so that I could no longer deny Him. I turned my life back over to the one who gave it to me and became born again.

My journey of healing began. I committed myself to reach optimal wellness in spirit, soul, and body. I studied the word of God daily, made prayer an ongoing conversation, and asked Him to purify my heart and free my mind.

I worked out, began eating healthier foods, cut down on my sugar intake, and started taking quality supplements. I saw a therapist and identified the reasons I turned to substances in the first place.

At the young age of five, I was introduced to masturbation at my babysitter's house, which led to secret sexual behaviors with friends throughout my adolescence. At age 12, my parents got divorced, which left a big wound in my heart.

When I discovered that turning to substances was my solution for coping with my childhood trauma, I was able to forgive others and myself and give it over to God. Slowly but surely, He healed the pain in my heart and gave me a peace that is irrespective of circumstances.

I learned there is no drink, drug, man, food, job, possession, or achievement that will ever be able to satisfy that craving inside of me. I found that God alone satisfies and helps us overcome.

I understand that you may not be an addict or follower of Jesus, but maybe you lack self-control or could use help overcoming an unhealthy habit.

Transformation is a process, not an event. Do not be discouraged. Transformation happened for me, and it can happen for you too! Take that leap and create Your Miracle Breakthrough!

If you are ready to give the world the best of you and not what is left of you, there is no better time than to start ASAP!

The ASAP Method to Create Your Miracle Breakthrough

A = Acknowledge *Your Unhealthy Habit*

Acknowledge your biggest unhealthy habit that you are ready to overcome. The first step to breaking through this habit is acknowledging the problem and having a real desire to change.

Some of the most common unhealthy habits are substance abuse, overeating, consuming too much sugar, constant worrying, procrastination, being a workaholic, sexual promiscuity, excessive use of social media, video games, pornography, lying, complaining, outbursts of anger, etc.

S= Surrender *Your Problem to God*

To gain freedom from your unhealthy habit, surrender it to God, whoever that may be for you. Tell Him your struggles and ask for His help. We are not meant to do life alone, but God gave us free will and will not intervene unless we seek His help. You don't have to hit rock bottom to fall to your knees. Humble yourself to God, and He will lift you up.

A= Act *Your Best and Let God Do the Rest!*

Take action and watch God help you overcome! God can't help or correct you if you are standing still. He'll work with you, but He won't do it for you. Before you act, make sure you pray and ask God to give you direction on how to move forward. Then listen and obey. Often God puts people and situations in our lives to help us, so be aware of opportunities that arise. You may feel inspired to join a program, hire a life coach, or see a therapist. You might already know what you need to do, but working with a coach or like-minded group will hold you accountable and dramatically increase your chances of success.

P= Persevere *Through Challenges*

TRAVEL LIGHT

At times you may be tempted to fall back into your old unhealthy habit... but you don't have to! When you feel tempted, remove yourself from the situation, pray, and then call an accountability partner. Don't let your feelings control you. Stay on course even when you don't feel like it. If you do make a mistake, admit it, ask for forgiveness, and start over. When you've been operating a certain way for so long, it takes time and perseverance to let old habits die. Keep going!

The ASAP method will lead you to your miracle breakthrough if you are willing to acknowledge your weaknesses, surrender and ask God for guidance, take action, and persevere!

Whatever path you take, I encourage you to invest in yourself. Give people the best of you, not what's left of you. Travel light.

Jennifer Evans

Jennifer Evans

Jennifer Evans is a Servant Leader, International Speaker, Transformational Coach, Actress, Show Host, and Humanitarian. She is dedicated to helping people create Miracle Breakthroughs so they can LIVE & GIVE their best lives.

Jennifer captivates audiences with her heart and humor, inspiring change through her powerful story of overcoming addiction, depression, anxiety, and burnout.

She is the Founder of Your Miracle Breakthrough transformational coaching, Host of The Jenerosity Show, and Founder of Jenerosity Foundation, a non-profit organization that empowers people to reach optimal wellness in spirit, soul, and body.

Jennifer served as a director for a public health charity where she developed programs in 45 countries on six continents, impacting hundreds of thousands of lives. She has served on a multitude of humanitarian missions with many high-profile people including President Bill Clinton, Elton John, Richard Branson, and Johnny Depp.

In her free time, Jennifer loves to spend time with God, play outdoors, and travel to new places. She is a graduate of the Walter Cronkite School of Journalism and Mass Communication at Arizona State University. Jennifer was born and raised in Mesa, Arizona and is currently enjoying life in sunny Los Angeles, California. Connect with Jennifer!

Email: jennifer@bejenerous.com
Social media: @JenerosityJen

CHAPTER 21

Ignite Your Fire
by Patrick Brown

I was born on the south side of Columbus, Ohio. At that time, we were a nuclear family with my dad, mom, older brother Calvin, and myself. My mom was a stay-at-home mom, and my dad was the #1 DJ on the radio in town.

From as far back as I can remember, my dad used to hold me in the air like in the Lion King and say, "Patrick, you were named after Patrice Lumumba, the great African warrior!" He said it with such intensity that I could feel it in my guts. It gave me a sense of pride that my dad bestowed such a great name upon me.

Pops was already well known throughout the city for his community activism and for being an outspoken, fast-talking DJ. It seemed like there was nowhere in the city of Columbus that they didn't know who my dad was. Back in those days, he was known as LB Triple P – Your Platter Playing Poppa! My dad was and is my hero. From his humble beginnings to the multitude of accolades and accomplishments, he has always seemed larger than life. If you haven't guessed by now, my dad is Les Brown.

My dad's popularity continued to grow as I got older. At this time, Muhammad Ali was 32 years old and the heavyweight champion of the world. My dad was on the radio, talking about how he used to be known for his fighting prowess. He said that he could beat Muhammad Ali in a fight.

The next thing I know, someone set up a sparring match between Muhammad Ali and my dad. They were to spar at East High School auditorium. I was nine years old at the time. I was excited to see the champ in person as were my brother and a couple hundred other spectators. Ali and pops were in suits. They put on boxing gloves and began to spar.

As I watched them, something overcame me. I was appalled that some man would have the audacity to hit my father. I became angrier and angrier with every passing second.

I started to get this jarring feeling in my guts. I leaned over to tell my big brother, the toughest guy I know, "We are going to have to go fight this guy for putting his hands on our dad." I saw my brother for the first and only time back down from a fight. He looked at me and said, "Are you crazy? He might have a Frazier or Foreman flashback."

I was shocked and disappointed at my brother's response, but that did not stop me. My dad was in a fight with the champ, and my big brother was not interested in facing the challenge. All I could think was, "I am a great African warrior! I am a warrior for my family. There was no choice; this man must feel my fury." This was my chance to defend the two greatest men in my life, my dad and my brother.

After Ali and my dad sparred for three to five minutes, my dad asked, "Is there anyone in the auditorium that would like to spar with the Champ?" No one in the auditorium moved but me. I immediately stood up and started walking towards the stage. I heard my father say, "I believe this is my nine-year-old son coming up here." I was thinking to myself, "Yes, Dad, I am coming. Patrick, the warrior of our family. Muhammad Ali had hit my dad. So he was going to have to hit me." I have what many would consider an old soul. I always considered myself a caregiver for my family.

I had a sense of responsibility for my dad's well-being. He gives and stands for others, and I stand for my dad and my family. I love my family more than anything. Nobody messes with my family, even if you're the heavyweight champion of the world! Ali punched the wrong one. There were going to be consequences for his actions.

I got on the stage. They gave me some gloves. I stood about five feet, seven inches tall, and 90 lbs. soaking wet with rocks in my pocket. I stood fearlessly with the eye of the tiger and fire in my gut to defend my family. I immediately started swinging a bunch of punches and commenced to whooping on the great Muhammad Ali himself.

Okay, it did not go exactly like that, but I did get a couple of good punches in. He dropped his hands and let me swing at the end. I swung until I couldn't anymore. He smirked at my intensity. He could see this was not just a sparring match for me. I was dead serious. I was in the ring to defend my dad as the warrior for my family. I did not win the fight, but I was the only person in the room beside my pops, willing even to dare to fight Muhammad Ali. I earned my dad and brother's respect that day.

A sense of self-worth was gained from doing what a room full of adults were unwilling to do. I learned to be courageous in the face of insurmountable odds. The love I have for my family ignites a fire in me. When you find what you are willing to sacrifice everything for, use it to fuel your dreams. Looking back, I am extremely proud and amazed at the courage and strength that I displayed.

Muhammad Ali was my biggest role model next to my dad. He always exemplified the same type of fire in his gut as I did. He was gregarious and passionate about life. That fire in his belly made him a legend. He trained relentlessly to become the greatest person to ever step in a boxing ring. He was adamant about proving the naysayers and critics wrong. He fearlessly and passionately proclaimed, "I am the greatest of all time!" long before he became the champ.

The day I fought Muhammad Ali was a defining moment in my life. I was braver than my elder brother and able to defend my father. I did not see a champion. I saw a man who put his hands on my dad.

I was elated because my father and brother admired how courageous I was and were impressed with me. I had solidified my role as the protector and crazy one of the family. I am a mild-mannered, very happy-go-lucky guy under normal circumstances. When it comes to my family, I am a warrior who is courageous and relentless for those I love.

It Is My Turn Now

It's been over 40 years since my fight with the champ. I have had many high and low points in my life since then. I have made more mistakes than I could even mention. I now find myself old enough to know better and way too old not to do better. My father is the elder statesman, and it is my time to move from the role of protector.

I had become comfortable being the protector of the family in the background admiring my dad. He worked incessantly in creating the results he desired. He has become one of the greatest orators of all time.

When you pursue things passionately and trust your gut feeling despite the opposition or obstacles you may be facing, that is where the impossible becomes possible. That "fire in your gut" resonates with the Divine and begins to manifest from the mental into the physical realm. What seems an impossible feat becomes light work.

You will begin to go outside yourself and face insurmountable odds to achieve your dream. Nothing great is accomplished without passion and a fire in your belly!

My New Dream

After years of admiring my father with his unceasing passion and fire in his gut to help others tap into their greatness, life comes full circle. Now I am called to step into the arena of my hero. I find myself facing one of the greatest of all time. It is one thing to fight the champ for my dad but to come into my dad's field where he is considered the best. I have tried to avoid this my whole life. There is no way I can compete against my dad. My time as a guardian has expired. I did not anticipate being called to come center stage and speak life to the masses. As intimidating and revered as I hold my dad, I now have someone more important who motivates me.

I have been blessed with two daughters and raising them has been both an honor and a privilege. My eldest daughter has blessed me with a grandchild. I thought to be a dad was great, but it pales in comparison to being a grandparent. You get to pour into the grandkids plenty of love, understanding, and fun. A dad in my eyes is supposed to exemplify the type of man you would like your daughters to find for themselves. Someone strong and self-assured while still being considerate and kind.

After raising my wonderful girls, I now have the reward of a grandson! I get to have all the fun and none of the responsibility. He is my bright-eyed, witty, ornery little man-man who thinks his pahpah is the coolest.

It was not until I was so proudly telling my grandson about who his great grandfather is and all of his achievements that I suddenly started having an uneasy feeling seep into my spirit. It jarred up a fighting spirit in me that I had not fully felt since I watched Muhammad Ali spar with my dad. These stories are great to share, but I have to be able to tell my grandson how I have helped to carry on the Brown family legacy.

With all of my dad's accomplishments in self-help and personal development, I felt I didn't need to be in the limelight. Or maybe it was the excuse I used so I would not have to come into the arena of the greatest orator of all time in my eyes.

Why attempt to fill the shoes of a giant, when you can stay in the background and get credit for being related to one? My grandson lit a fire in my guts to be a trailblazer in my own right – that same fire and spark Ali had in his belly and eyes when he fought his way up the ranks in boxing. The same fire that my dad has in his belly for uplifting people through his message of hope and empowerment. I now have someone watching me, and quitting was no longer an option.

There is nothing I would not do to be an excellent example for my grandson. I am going to tell my grandson what a significant impact his grandfather has made on society, not just who his great grandfather is. My soul demands that I push through any self-doubt or fear.

My grandson is watching, and I must show him how to manifest his greatness through my example. I recognize I am not the great Les Brown. That no longer has any bearing on my life. I have a voice and something of value to share. I will be the best me I know how to be. I will do it passionately to be an inspiration to my grandson.

One of the steps I have taken to further the Brown legacy is collecting a lifetime of mentorship from my dad and all my training, work experiences, life lessons, and designing a program to prepare people to be relevant in this new virtual market.

I started a new company and our motto is, "Live in the moment for the moment is all we have." I am now a speaker and trainer. My team has researched cutting edge organizations and learned what it takes to be a leader in most industries in the age of automation and the new millennial mindset. Our team is dedicated to helping shape the great voices and impactful leaders of this new generation.

Our main objective is to educate people of their heritage of greatness, enlighten them to possibility thinking, and inspire them to take action to live their dreams. I believe that we all are put here to leave the world a little bit better off than when we arrived. It is essential to find that someone or something that ignites a fire in your gut. You must find the warrior within yourself to get tunnel vision and focus on conquering whomever or whatever prevents you from living your best life.

What or who ignites the fire in you? Is there anything that you are willing to give your all to, no matter the outcome? If you don't know what it is, you need to find it. We all have a fire buried deep in our gut. You need to find what ignites it for you.

If I could leave you with anything, it would be these three things:

- It doesn't matter who your family, friends, or associates may be. It is up to you to decide to live YOUR dreams.
- Sometimes life causes us to bury that fire deep inside of us. You may think it is gone, but it is not. There is still a tiny ember inside of you waiting to be fanned into a flame.
- Think of the legacy you are going to leave. What is your family going to say about you when you are gone?

There is a fire in my spirit now that cannot be put out. I am ready for the new path ahead and excited for where it leads. I want to encourage you to ignite the fire in your soul. There is no greater feeling than living life passionately and realizing your dreams!!!

Patrick Brown

Patrick Brown

Patrick W. Brown is the owner of Preparing For Tomorrow Inc. He is a member of The First Family of Motivation and second eldest son of world-renowned motivational speaker Les Brown.

Patrick is a licensed facilitator of LifeSpring, Certified Youth Leadership trainer, Ty Cobb certified speaker, Certified in DISC, and also a Les Brown speaker/trainer and coach. Patrick has also developed his own training on Leadership: Leading out Loud-New Millennium Leadership.

Patrick has a great mentor in his father, Les Brown. "The greatest thing my father has taught me is the importance of living a life of service."

He utilizes poetry, acting, and humor to create an experience to help shift the mindset. One of his favorite sayings is, "I talk into the heart to unlock the mind. I share my life experiences to educate and inspire people to live out their dreams." Patrick Brown would love to collaborate with you and your team to customize a speech for your business, organization, or non-profit.

www.PreparingForTomorrowINC.com

ACKNOWLEDGEMENTS

I would like to acknowledge my mother, Phyllis M. Nutter, for giving me life and my father, Les Brown, for giving me direction and purpose.

I am so grateful for the ability to do what I love... and experience each unfolding day as a magnificent and mysterious ride. I have been blessed with countless angels... here are just a few:

Mama Corrine Jefferson	Dr. Cindy Trimm
Jessie Willams	Dr. Maya Angelou
Monica M. Brooks	Oprah Winfrey
Dr. Johnnie Colemon	Michelle Obama
Mia Michaux	Mark Armstrong
Irvin P. Williams	Dr. Cheryl D. George
Leatha Lightsey	Kim Thompson-Pinder
Tim Byrd	Raymond Harlall
Lamont Smith	John-Leslie Brown
Rev. Michael Kelly	Riadh Hamdi
Dr. Barbara King	Mary Anderson
Naima Clarke (Lil Cuzin)	Valdez Henry
Alphonso Jackson	Yusef & Sanovia Salaam
Kountry Wayne	Reverend Kevin Ross
Bishop T.D. Jakes	(Rev Kev)
First Lady Serrita Jakes	Dr. Mark Armstrong